Cambridge Elements

Elements of Christianity and Science
edited by
Andrew Davison
University of Cambridge

CHRISTIANITY AND AGROECOLOGY

Matthew Philipp Whelan
Duke University

Shaftesbury Road, Cambridge CB2 8EA, United Kingdom

One Liberty Plaza, 20th Floor, New York, NY 10006, USA

477 Williamstown Road, Port Melbourne, VIC 3207, Australia

314–321, 3rd Floor, Plot 3, Splendor Forum, Jasola District Centre, New Delhi – 110025, India

103 Penang Road, #05–06/07, Visioncrest Commercial, Singapore 238467

Cambridge University Press is part of Cambridge University Press & Assessment, a department of the University of Cambridge.

We share the University's mission to contribute to society through the pursuit of education, learning and research at the highest international levels of excellence.

www.cambridge.org
Information on this title: www.cambridge.org/9781009547796
DOI: 10.1017/9781009158213

© Matthew Philipp Whelan 2025

This publication is in copyright. Subject to statutory exception and to the provisions of relevant collective licensing agreements, no reproduction of any part may take place without the written permission of Cambridge University Press & Assessment.

When citing this work, please include a reference to the DOI 10.1017/9781009158213

First published 2025

A catalogue record for this publication is available from the British Library

ISBN 978-1-009-54779-6 Hardback
ISBN 978-1-009-15822-0 Paperback
ISSN 2634-3460 (online)
ISSN 2634-3452 (print)

Cambridge University Press & Assessment has no responsibility for the persistence or accuracy of URLs for external or third-party internet websites referred to in this publication and does not guarantee that any content on such websites is, or will remain, accurate or appropriate.

For EU product safety concerns, contact us at Calle de José Abascal, 56, 1°, 28003 Madrid, Spain, or email eugpsr@cambridge.org

Christianity and Agroecology

Elements of Christianity and Science

DOI: 10.1017/9781009158213
First published online: May 2025

Matthew Philipp Whelan
Duke University

Author for correspondence: Matthew Philipp Whelan,
matthew.whelan@duke.edu

Abstract: This Element draws on the transdisciplinary field of agroecology to clarify and deepen Catholic social teaching's natural law ethic. In response to the ecological crisis, social teaching has begun to appeal to ecology and the exemplarity of natural ecosystems to foster care of creation. Some have criticized this natural law ethic, along with its invocations of balance and harmony, as overly idealized, advocating instead for an alternative view in which ecological dynamism and ambiguity preclude appeals to ecology for guidance. While sympathizing with these criticisms, this Element offers a different way forward, contending that social teaching's natural law ethic should be revised rather than abandoned. Agroecology displays an approach to tilling and keeping the earth that accommodates dynamism and ambiguity, while also discerning ecological principles and processes that are mimicked agriculturally. In short, this Element argues that engaging agroecology can help social teaching clarify, concretize, and deepen its understanding of natural law.

Keywords: Catholic social teaching, agroecology, environmental ethics, natural law, Laudato si'

© Matthew Philipp Whelan 2025

ISBNs: 9781009547796 (HB), 9781009158220 (PB), 9781009158213 (OC)
ISSNs: 2634-3460 (online), 2634-3452 (print)

Contents

1 Agroecology, Natural Law, and Catholic Social Teaching   1

2 A Tilling That Keeps   15

3 Toward a Deeper Understanding of the Natural Law   35

4 Science-Engaged Theology and Theologically-Engaged Science   50

   Bibliography   65

1 Agroecology, Natural Law, and Catholic Social Teaching

Introduction

How do we provide for ourselves and for one another while also preserving the land and other sources that make our provisioning possible? The question is a human one, implicating all people on this planet. It is also an inescapably agricultural one. "No matter how urban our life," the American writer, farmer, and activist Wendell Berry observes, "our bodies live by farming; we come from the earth and return to it, and so we live in agriculture as we live in flesh."[1]

When it comes to the treatment of people and the use of the world, few human activities are as consequential as our eating and the agriculture that supports it. In recent decades, the issue of agricultural provisioning has become increasingly urgent due to the widespread recognition that the dominant approach – modern industrial agriculture – is in crisis. There is a growing consensus that we are at a crossroads and must find alternatives.

Agroecology has emerged as a promising alternative. It is a discipline that integrates ecological principles and processes into the design and management of agricultural systems (otherwise known as agroecosystems). In his book *Agroecology: The Science of Sustainable Agriculture*, a pioneering and programmatic text in the field, Miguel Altieri describes agroecology as an attempt "to reinstate a more ecological rationale into agricultural production," an approach that is based on "a deep understanding of the nature of agroecosystems and the principles by which they function." The result is an agriculture that is both "productive and natural resource conserving," while also being "culturally sensitive, socially just, and economically viable."[2] Agroecologists like Altieri believe that it is possible to provide for ourselves and for one another while also preserving the land and other sources of provisioning, emphasizing that doing so requires working with the ecological principles and processes that enable and sustain creaturely life on this planet.

Agroecology has garnered widespread global support from scientific groups, intergovernmental initiatives, and international agencies and organizations. It is regarded by these entities as crucial to strategies of agricultural transformation and adaptation in response to a future marked by higher temperatures, extreme weather events, and unpredictable climatic conditions.[3] However, despite this support, agroecology and its significance for our agricultural provisioning have

---

[1] Berry, *The Unsettling of America*, 101.   [2] Altieri, *Agroecology*, ix.
[3] International Assessment of Agricultural Knowledge, Science, and Technology for Development, *Agriculture at a Crossroads*; Intergovernmental Panel on Climate Change, *Climate Change and Land*; International Panel of Experts on Sustainable Food Systems, "From Uniformity to Diversity"; High Level Panel of Experts on Food Security and Nutrition, "Agroecological and Other Innovative Approaches"; Schutter, "Agroecology and the Right to Food."

yet to impact significantly the field of Christian theology and ethics. This Element aims to address this lacuna, contending that theologians and ethicists have much to learn from it.

The question of how we provide for ourselves and one another while also preserving the sources of such provisioning is not just a human and agricultural one but also resonates with Christians and all those who abide by the original human vocation "to till and keep" the garden of the world (Gen. 2:15; see also *Gaudium et spes*, no. 1).[4] Writing out of the Catholic social teaching tradition – a moral theological tradition that consistently appeals to this same passage from Genesis to describe the human vocation[5] – Pope Francis in *Laudato si'* (2015) explains that while tilling conveys cultivating, working, and making use of God's creation to meet our legitimate needs, keeping evokes care, protection, and preservation as we do so. "This implies a relationship of mutual responsibility between human beings and nature.[6] Each community can take from the bounty of the earth whatever it needs for subsistence, but it also has the duty to protect the earth and to ensure its fruitfulness for coming generations" (no. 67). For Francis and for Catholic social teaching, as well as for Christian theologians and ethicists more generally, rediscovering this vocation is essential to caring for the world we share with God's other creatures.

In arguing that agroecology can help Christians and people of good will better realize their vocation to till and keep the garden of the world, I focus on the Catholic social teaching tradition in particular. My goal is to display agroecology's theological resonances and follow those who have already taken up agroecology as a tool for evangelization.[7] However, I also argue that agroecology is not a tool that Christians can employ without being transformed in the process. As we will see in our examination of Catholic social teaching, constructive engagement with agroecology illuminates deficiencies in the tradition's natural law ethic, particularly regarding its understanding of ecology. Yet, agroecology offers wisdom that can help repair these deficiencies. Thus, agroecology not only highlights problems in social teaching's understanding of ecology but also presents opportunities for renovation and renewal. At the

---

[4] Unless otherwise indicated, all documents related to Catholic social teaching can be found at www.vatican.va. Norman Wirzba has reflected profoundly on this vocation in *Food and Faith*.
[5] John Paul II, *Sollicitudo rei socialis*, nos. 29–30; Benedict XVI, *Caritas in veritate*, no. 48.
[6] Rather than "nature," "environment," or even "ecology," contemporary Catholic social teaching relies most fundamentally on the language of creation to describe the mysterious bonds uniting humans with the rest of creation and the care these bonds require. As Francis explains, "the word 'creation' has a broader meaning than 'nature'" – and the same applies to terms like "environment" and "ecology" (*Laudato si'*, nos. 76, 139). Therefore, when employing these terms, the tradition reshapes them in light of the language of creation.
[7] Specific examples of Christian-inspired agroecological initiatives can be found in Whelan, *Theological Foundations for Agriculture According to Laudato si'*, 35–38.

same time, while this Element focuses in particular on agroecology's contribution to social teaching, it aims to foster a genuine conversation. Therefore, in addition to demonstrating how engagement with agroecology can repair and renew Catholic social teaching, I also show how a moral theological tradition like social teaching can clarify and deepen agroecology, helping to surface the discipline's larger metaphysical stakes.

Natural Law

The question of how we provision agriculturally for ourselves and one another without degrading the sources of our provisioning relates to what the Christian tradition has historically called natural law. As we will see, there is a close relationship between natural law and the participation of the human creature in God's providential care for creation. In recent years, a number of scholars have attempted a critical retrieval of natural law for Christian ecological theology and ethics.[8] This Element builds on such work by exploring the implications of that retrieval for agriculture, demonstrating how natural law reflection can constructively engage sciences like ecology and agronomy, as well as transdisciplinary fields like agroecology.

Given the diverse accounts of natural law both within and outside Christianity, it is essential to clarify my own understanding. Thomas Aquinas, an important voice in what follows, offers this helpful definition in the *Summa theologiae*, underscoring the close relationship between natural law, God's work of providential care for creation, and the human creature's participation in this care:

> It is evident that all things participate in eternal law [the eternal law is the divine wisdom directing the actions and movements of all creatures toward their end], in that their tendencies to their own proper acts and ends are from its impression. Among them, rational creatures are subject to divine providence in a more excellent way, insofar as they participate in providence by their own providing for themselves and others. Thus, they join in and make their own the eternal reason through which they have their natural aptitudes for their due activity and purpose. And such sharing in the eternal law by rational creatures is called the natural law.[9]

A number of aspects of Thomas's account in this passage are important for my own approach. While I only note these aspects briefly now, we will return to them as the argument unfolds.

---

[8] Northcott, *The Environment and Christian Ethics*; Nash, "Seeking Moral Norms in Nature"; Traina, "Response to Nash."

[9] Thomas Aquinas, *Summa theologiae*, I-II.91.2 resp. Translation slightly altered.

- *Natural law is a theological form of reflection that locates human morality within a wider landscape. It has an especially intimate relation to God's creation of all things visible and invisible, as well as God's providential care for creation.* Providence (from the Latin *providere*, meaning "look ahead," "prepare," "supply," "make provision") implies acting for an end, in this case, the Creator's provisioning of what creatures need (see Gen 1:29–30; Ps 104:27). It is crucial to clarify that not all accounts of natural law are the same. The account offered in these pages differs from one that emerged in modernity, where natural law names a rational, secular, and universal moral code, yielding a straightforward and unambiguous account of human nature and, by extension, the natural world.[10] In contrast, the theological account offered here does not derive moral norms from reason alone, as Hugo Grotius, Thomas Hobbes, and John Locke do. Instead, it places us in a complex process of discernment regarding the kinds of creatures we are and the creation we inhabit, a process that presumes our participation in and formation by communities. The account of natural law here is also shaped by scriptural and theological sources, while remaining open to wisdom from outside, including the sciences. However, this openness does not imply this account of natural law is insufficiently theological, as creation is a theological category. As Jean Porter reminds us, "not everything that is properly Christian is uniquely Christian."[11]
- *Natural law implicates the entirety of creation, along with its characteristic traits such as goodness, wisdom, intelligibility, and integrity.* For Thomas, all things are good by virtue of being created, and they also share in God's providential wisdom, a sharing he associates with their being and acting as the creatures they are. By so being and acting, creatures convey the discernable impress of divine wisdom, even if imperfectly. Accordingly, natural law presumes an integrity to creation and implies that creation can be analyzed in terms of its own intelligible principles of operation. While natural law implicates the human creature in distinctive ways, it also closely relates to the belief that creation is God's good gift, and that creation reflects the Wisdom that made it and in which it holds together.[12] To cite Porter again, natural law therefore does not drive a "wedge" between human creatures and the wider creation, and it perceives human reason and activities like moral discernment as expressions of a more pervasive reality of creaturely participation in God's providential wisdom.[13]

---

[10] Porter, *Nature as Reason*, 26–27. [11] Porter, *Nature as Reason*, 65.
[12] Edwards, *Jesus the Wisdom of God*. [13] Porter, *Nature as Reason*, 49.

- *Natural law implicates the human creature in distinctive ways.* Humans, like all creatures, participate in God's providence, but we do so differently from other creatures. Despite its limitations, current discourse on the Anthropocene – atmospheric chemist Paul Crutzen's term for a novel planetary condition in which humankind's power and influence pervade and fundamentally alter earth's systems – points to this distinctiveness.[14] The Anthropocene refers not only to the power (certain) humans have had over planetary life but also to how that power has been wielded willfully, as well as to how its consequences are interpreted. The Anthropocene raises questions, such as, will we take responsibility for what is happening and develop new forms of solidarity in the face of present and future devastations? Regardless of what we name it – Anthropocene, Capitolocene, Plantationocene, or something else[15] – this condition implicates our capability to discern the kinds of creatures we are and the world we inhabit, as well as to reason morally in light of those discernments. As Francis observes in *Laudato si'*, we are creatures capable of responding to the "message contained in the structures of nature itself" (no. 117) – just as we are also capable of disregarding it. Regarding natural law, an important exemplification of humankind's distinctive creaturely agency is our ability to profess faith in God's providential care for creation, opting to take that care as the law for our own lives. As Thomas notes, providing for ourselves and others as God does – conforming, we might say, our provisioning to God's – epitomizes human participation in God's providence. For all those who claim that Jesus Christ is the very flesh of that providential care, it is fitting that we should strive to imitate that care in our relationships with one another and with the wider creaturely world.
- *"By natural law, all things are common."* Although not explicitly mentioned earlier, this claim from Gratian's *Decretum* about natural law – that God gives creation as a common gift, meant for the use and enjoyment of all people – is axiomatic to Thomas's thought and essential to how he thinks our provisioning conforms to God's.[16] According to Thomas, conformity requires managing what we possess not simply for ourselves alone but as if it is common, given for the use and enjoyment of all people. The evidence of such management is a willingness to share what we have with others, especially with those who are in need of basic goods like food, drink, shelter, clothing, and medicine.[17] We see this same claim about creation's commonality reflected in a more explicitly ecological register in *Laudato si'* when Francis describes

---

[14] Crutzen and Stoermer, "The Anthropocene." Regarding the limitations of this discourse, see Malm and Hornborg, "The Geology of Mankind?"

[15] Haraway, "Anthropocene, Capitalocene, Plantationocene, Chthulucene."

[16] Reyes, "By Nature Common."   [17] Aquinas, *Summa theologiae*, II-II.62.2.

our duty to keep the earth and to ensure its fruitfulness for the use of future generations, in which the commonality of the gift unfolds across time.

Catholic Social Teaching

What follows is an engagement with agroecology from the vantage of this broadly Thomistic account of natural law,[18] particularly this account's integration into and development within the tradition of Catholic social teaching. One rationale for this approach, apart from my own commitment to the tradition, stems from developments in the field of theology and science. Recently, there has been a salutary shift in focus from attention to methodological questions – for instance, regarding the relationship between religion/theology and science – to more granular analyses of how specific scientific findings or theological questions inform each other. This new emphasis on granularity and specificity, known as science-engaged theology, enables science to become a more generative source for theological reasoning and underpins my focus on Catholic social teaching in this volume.[19] Another, related rationale for my approach is the widespread readership, admiration, and study of social teaching, even among those who are not Catholic, bolstering the hope that my engagement with agroecology, while situated within a particular tradition, might resonate beyond it.

Deeply rooted in scripture and Christian history, Catholic social teaching assumed its modern form in the late nineteenth century in response to the upheavals of the Industrial Revolution. Modern social teaching is often thought to begin with the pontificate of Leo XIII and his 1891 encyclical *Rerum novarum*. In this document, Leo sought to imagine and enact justice amid the turmoil of industrialism, illuminating social life with the light of the Gospel.[20] Over time, subsequent contributions built on Leo's, developing an inner logic and coherence that gradually became a unified body of teaching or doctrine related to social life. Notably, Thomas Aquinas has had a significant formative influence on this tradition.[21]

The point of departure for this Element is Catholic social teaching's response to the damage we have done to our common home, to allude to Francis's

---

[18] For more on this broadly Thomistic account, in addition to Porter, see also French, "Natural Law and Ecological Responsibility"; Cahill, *Global Justice, Christology and Christian Ethics*, 247–289.
[19] See Joanna Leidenhag and John Perry, "Science-Engaged Theology"; Davison, "Science and Specificity."
[20] See Whelan, *Blood in the Fields*, 85–139.
[21] Finnis, "Aquinas as a Primary Source of Catholic Social Teaching."

formulation in *Laudato si'* (no. 63).²² This response has led to an ecologization of social teaching and its natural law ethic. The International Theological Commission (ITC) in *In Search of a Universal Ethic: A New Look at the Natural Law* (2009) describes this process of ecologization, stating, "There cannot be an adequate response to the complex questions of ecology, except within the framework of a deeper understanding of the natural law, which places value on the connection between the human person, society, culture, and the equilibrium of the bio-physical sphere in which the human person is incarnate."²³

The ITC refers to this deeper understanding of natural law as an "integral ecology" – a concept central to *Laudato si'* and Francis's call for an ecology responsive to the damage we have done (no. 63). Social teaching's natural law ethic and integral ecology are therefore largely synonymous and used interchangeably in what follows. The word "integral" comes from the Latin *integralis* for "forming a whole." In the case of integral ecology, the ecological 'whole' incorporates three fundamental and interconnected relationships that are the foundation of human life on this earth: our relationship with God, with one another, and with the wider creaturely world (no. 66). These relationships are fundamental because we cannot escape them, and they are interconnected because changes in one inevitably lead to changes in the others. By incorporating these three relationships, integral ecology stretches and transforms ecology beyond its usual meaning – but not beyond the semantic range conveyed by the word's own etymology (*Ökologie* from Greek *oikos* "house, dwelling place, habitation" and *logia* "study of") and history of usage.²⁴

Within the context of these developments, Catholic social teaching appeals to a wisdom in the wider creaturely world for practical guidance on our good use of it – an appeal that is at the heart of its ecologized natural law ethic. In *Caritas in veritate* (2009), Pope Benedict XVI writes of creation's "intrinsic balance" and "inbuilt order" from which we can draw "the principles needed in order 'to till and keep it' [Gen 2:15]." Nature, he continues, "is a wondrous work of the Creator containing a 'grammar' which sets forth ends and criteria for its wise use" (no. 48). Following Benedict, Pope Francis similarly appeals to this "grammar."²⁵ Contrasting the dominant industrial system and its "throwaway culture" with how natural ecosystems absorb and reuse by-products, Francis urges the development of models of production and forms of economic life that

---

[22] An overview of Catholic social teaching's ecologization can be found in Deane-Drummond, "Joining in the Dance" and Whelan, "Care for Creation, Environmentalism, and Ecology."
[23] ITC, *In Search of a Universal Ethic*, sec. 3.4.82.   [24] Worster, *Nature's Economy*.
[25] Francis, "Fraternity, the Foundation and Pathway to Peace."

mimic the "balance" and "harmony" of ecosystems (*Laudato si'* nos. 22, 35, 57, 224).

Despite Benedict and Francis's laudable efforts, significant and unresolved issues remain regarding the ecologization of Catholic social teaching. While *Laudato si'* breaks new ground by taking ecology and other sciences into account in novel ways,[26] the passages just quoted indicate that the ecologization pursued by Francis, like those pursued by ITC and Benedict before him, is only partial. Social teaching consistently employs the language of equilibrium, balance, and harmony to describe the natural world, as well as its diverse array of creatures and processes. As a consequence, Celia Deane-Drummond and others have rightly noted a jarring dissonance between social teaching and the best scientific knowledge we have. The result, as Deane-Drummond puts it, is "an idealized view of natural, stable, harmonious ecology rather than a recognition either of suffering ... or fluid and dynamic ecological processes."[27]

Adherents and scholars of Catholic social teaching might respond to this critique by appealing to Francis's contention in *Laudato si'* that integral ecology draws on the sciences without being reduced to them. Throughout the encyclical, Francis argues that we cannot develop an ecology capable of remedying the damage we have done without extra-scientific forms of wisdom, including moral theological traditions like social teaching. In other words, the development of an integral ecology seeks to resist scientific reductionism and to open up the sciences to a broader vision of reality that many sciences currently lack (nos. 62–63, 138, 141, 143, 159). However, the issue Deane-Drummond raises is different and calls for a response: it is whether integral ecology can avoid scientific reductionism while also retaining scientific accountability. One of the crucial issues at stake in this Element is what further revisions of natural law such accountability entails.

Another related issue is widespread skepticism in contemporary theology regarding natural law. In light of concerns like Deane-Drummond's and empirical realities such as fluid and dynamic ecological processes, as well as the role of death in ecological systems, we will encounter some who suggest that accountability to the sciences and to empirical reality problematizes any construal of natural law altogether. In other words, a more complete ecologization yields an understanding of the creaturely world that conveys no message and offers no guidance for how we should live.

Given all these issues, my primary purpose in this Element is twofold. First, it is to introduce Christians and people of good will to agroecology and help them

---

[26] Deane-Drummond, "*Laudato si'* and the Natural Sciences."
[27] Deane-Drummond, "Joining in the Dance," 211.

recognize the resonances between their own commitments and agroecology's particular approach to agriculture. Agroecology teaches us about our vocation to till and keep the earth, offering practical tools to provide for ourselves and for one another. Regarding the specific moral theological tradition under consideration here, Catholic social teaching claims its account of natural law has concrete implications for our care of creation, and I argue that agroecology has an important role to play in realizing those implications and assisting the church in its evangelizing task. Second, and closely related, my other main purpose is to display for adherents and scholars of Catholic social teaching how they can learn from disciplines like agroecology – not just in terms of practical application of their natural law ethic. Agroecology also offers them wisdom to address unresolved issues regarding their tradition's own conception of integral ecology. In so doing, agroecology can contribute to the clarification and even development of social teaching's natural law ethic, ecologizing and deepening it still further.

Agroecology

Because this Element belongs to a series in Christianity and science, a further word of introduction to agroecology is necessary, particularly regarding the kind of discipline it is, how it emerged, and its recognition today as a science, a practice, and a politics. While agroecology certainly incorporates the agricultural sciences, it is transdisciplinary, drawing on forms of knowledge beyond science alone.[28] Agroecology's overarching goal is to develop, in a particular locale, an agriculture that preserves and works with the sources that sustain it. Achieving this goal requires methodologies and collaborative processes involving multiple researchers, practitioners, and other actors.[29] For these and other reasons, agroecology is not a typical interlocutor in the dialogue between Christianity and science.

Agroecology emerged in the early decades of the twentieth century as a science combining both agronomy and ecology.[30] While modern agronomy originated in the mid-nineteenth century as an applied science harnessing advances in soil chemistry and plant breeding to increase crop production, ecology emerged later in the century and mostly focused on natural systems apart from any practical applications for human life. Throughout much of the twentieth century, agronomy and ecology largely developed separately from

---

[28] Russell, Wickson, and Carew, "Transdisciplinarity."
[29] High Level Panel of Experts on Food Security and Nutrition, "Agroecological and Other Innovative Approaches," 33.
[30] This paragraph draws on Gliessman et al., *Agroecology*, 29–31; Wezel et al., "Agroecology as a Science, a Movement and a Practice," 503–505.

one another. In contrast, from its inception, agroecology sought their integration, primarily in response to what agroecologists regarded as the deleterious consequences of agricultural science's increasing subservience to "the industrial ideal," in Deborah Fitzgerald's apt formulation.[31]

The Russian agronomist Basil Bensin, who first coined the term "agroecology," defined it as a research program that bases agriculture on ecology rather than industry.[32] Although Rachel Carson did not call herself an agroecologist, she followed this same line, arguing in *Silent Spring* that industrial agriculture fails to recognize and learn from ecological principles and processes, instead imposing its profit-driven logic on the world in the form of extensive monocultures and exclusive reliance on chemical control of insect herbivores. Throughout the book, Carson examines the scientific basis for an alternative approach that, in contrast to industrial agriculture, takes advantage of these ecological principles and processes by developing polycultures that maintain and enhance biodiversity, as well as by mimicking predator–prey dynamics through strategies of biological control of insect herbivores.[33] This alternative approach is agroecology.

As agroecology continued to evolve over the course of the twentieth century, it retained its scientific roots, studying agroecosystems and the ecological principles and processes within them. However, additional aspects of the discipline began to emerge, especially as agroecological scientists recognized that smallholder agricultural systems throughout the world – systems managed by peasants, indigenous peoples, hunters and gatherers, family farmers, herders and pastoralists, and others – already practiced an agriculture based on ecology rather than industry.[34] Indeed, one reason these systems existed was because the smallholders' very marginality forced them to rely on their locale and work with ecological principles and processes within it. Such smallholders were unable to afford the expensive equipment and purchased inputs that larger wealthier farmers could. Consequently, the agricultural systems these smallholders inherited and developed embodied what agroecological scientists sought, offering living laboratories for the development of agroecosystems and management practices. More and more, agroecological scientists studied these systems and collaborated with farmers to understand, support, and improve them.[35]

---

[31] Fitzgerald, *Every Farm a Factory*.
[32] Bensin, "Possibilities for International Cooperation in Agroecology Investigation."
[33] Carson, *Silent Spring*, 10.
[34] Toledo, "The Ecological Rationality of Peasant Production"; Toledo and Barrera-Bassols, *La Memoria Biocultural*; Koohafkan and Altieri, *Globally Important Agricultural Heritage Systems*.
[35] Altieri, "Why Study Traditional Agriculture?"; Toledo, "The Ecological Rationality of Peasant Production"; Shiva, *Who Really Feeds the World?*

An important gathering of these same smallholders, along with diverse organizations and movements representing them, occurred in Nyéléni, Mali, in 2015, exemplifying the importance of agroecology as a practice, as well as a science. The participants state in their declaration that "our ancestral production systems have been developed over millennia, and during the past thirty to forty years, this has come to be called agroecology."[36] They observe that the production practices of these ancestral systems derive from "ecological principles like building life in the soil, recycling nutrients, and the dynamic management of biodiversity and energy conservation at all scales."[37]

Yet, despite existing on marginal lands – typically too hilly or mountainous, or lands that have thin or infertile soil, or both – with little potential for modern industrial agriculture, and in communities with limited access to roads, markets, transportation, capital, or governmental support, these agricultural systems nevertheless make an enormous and underappreciated contribution to feeding the world, as found by the UN.'s Food and Agriculture Organization (FAO) and others. For instance, a recent and comprehensive study reported that while small farms (defined as less than two hectares or about five acres) constitute about 84 percent of all farms and occupy about 12 percent of all agricultural land, they currently produce about 35 percent of the world's food. If we broaden our view, family farms – which can be of various sizes and management regimes, including industrial – account for about 90 percent of all farms, occupy approximately 70–80 percent of all agricultural land, and produce around 80 percent of the world's food.[38] The reality to which these figures point considerably complicates the oft-repeated and widely held claims that industrial agriculture alone feeds the world, that it alone can do so, and that advocating for alternatives is fantasy.[39]

We have been focusing on the emergence of agroecological science and practice as two important aspects of the discipline of agroecology as it is understood today, but the Nyéléni gathering itself also points to a third aspect: agroecology as a politics. The participants at Nyéléni articulate agroecological politics in stark terms: "We see agroecology as a key form of resistance to an economic system that puts profit before life."[40] Industrial agriculture, they argue, "destroys soil fertility, is responsible for the deforestation of rural

---

[36] "Declaration of the International Forum for Agroecology," 163.
[37] "Declaration of the International Forum for Agroecology," 165.
[38] See Lowder, Sánchez, and Bertini, "Which Farms Feed the World and Has Farmland Become More Concentrated?"; Agriculture and Economic Development Analysis Division, *The State of Food and Agriculture*; Ricciardi et al., "How Much of the World's Food Do Smallholders Produce?"
[39] A classic argument against these "myths" is Lappé and Collins, *World Hunger*, 67–130.
[40] "Declaration of the International Forum for Agroecology," 164.

areas, the contamination of water, and the acidification of oceans and the killing of fisheries," in addition to fueling climate change. They also note that the advance of industrial agriculture is closely tied to land grabbing,[41] the criminalization of social movements, the commodification of essential goods of agricultural production like seeds, and the adverse health effects of heavily processed foods.[42]

What does prioritizing life over profit look like? Those at Nyéléni describe agroecological politics as a "joint struggle for justice" – a justice that is simultaneously social and ecological, implicating human and non-human life alike.[43] For the delegates, this justice is embodied in agricultural systems that work with ecological principles and processes by cultivating biodiversity, establishing habitable spaces for other creatures, and sustaining the natural sources of agricultural productivity. At the same time, this justice involves defending and supporting the peoples and communities that continue to cultivate these agricultural systems. The delegates use the phrase "food sovereignty" to describe the conditions under which this justice can be realized. The phrase refers to the ability of peoples and communities to continue to exist and maintain relationships with their land, necessitating recognition of their laws, traditions, customs, land tenure systems, and institutions. Food sovereignty also involves putting "the control of seeds, biodiversity, land and territories, waters, [and] knowledge ... in the hands of the peoples who feed the world."[44]

The developments just sketched help us to appreciate why agroecology is often defined today as a science, a practice, and a politics.[45] "Although each of these aspects of agroecology is critical," explains Stephen Gliessman, "their integration is what forms the framework for food system transformation."[46] Agroecology asserts that this transformation requires more and better *science* on the ecological principles and processes within agroecosystems. It also necessitates the *practice* of an agriculture modeled on ecology, not industry, and supporting the peoples and communities that actually enact it. Finally, this transformation demands a *politics* that advocates for agroecology in a world whose structures, institutions, policies, and laws often undermine or militate

---

[41] These are large-scale land acquisitions, often by foreign investors, in the Global South that have already dispossessed many. See Nolte, Chamberlain, and Giger, "International Land Deals for Agriculture"; Yang and He, "Global Land Grabbing."
[42] "Declaration of the International Forum for Agroecology," 164–165.
[43] "Declaration of the International Forum for Agroecology," 163."
[44] "Declaration of the International Forum for Agroecology," 165–166.
[45] See High Level Panel of Experts on Food Security and Nutrition, "Agroecological and Other Innovative Approaches," 31–39.
[46] See Gliessman, "Defining Agroecology," 600.

against it. In short, agroecological science, practice, and politics are all essential to bringing into being a world that truly prioritizes life over profit.

What results from the integration of agroecological science, practice, and politics is a different vision of the world and our place within it compared to the specialized agricultural science associated with industrial agriculture. John Vandermeer articulates these differences in terms of "the two cultures of agricultural science: that of the agronomist (and other classical agricultural disciplines such as horticulture and entomology) and that of the ecologist (or agroecologist)." For Vandermeer, the key difference between these cultures lies in the questions they ask. Whereas the agronomist's characteristic question is, *what are the problems the farmer faces, and how can I help solve them?* the ecologist-agroecologist's is, *why are things that could be problems in the agroecosystem not problems?* In other words, the agronomist sees a sick farm needing treatment, while the ecologist-agroecologist sees a (potentially) flourishing farm that integrates so well with ecological principles and process that issues with insect herbivores, diseases, and soil fertility seldom arise in the first place.[47]

Some observers have critiqued agroecology's integration of science, practice, and politics, suggesting that it would be better for the discipline to understand itself as a science alone.[48] The critique stems from at least three widespread and interrelated presumptions about science that agroecology challenges and that are important to signal here. The first is that science is the truest kind of knowledge and serves as the standard for all rationality. The second presumption is that science pursues a value-free ideal and that normativity has no place within it. The third and final one is that, because science serves as the standard for rationality, agroecology's attempt to integrate science, practice, and politics is a mistake and dilutes the discipline's contribution to knowledge.

Agroecology challenges these presumptions by drawing on diverse forms of rationality and ways of knowing, including, but not limited to, science. In this way, agroecology stands as a countercurrent to the imposing, authoritative voice that agricultural science can sometimes assume, especially in the Global South, where the power differential between science and those who receive its deliverances is especially pronounced.[49] Relatedly, agroecological science, like agroecology more generally, is ordered by a normative vision of an agrifood system patterned on ecology rather than industry. Agroecology thus helps us see that science, like other forms of human agency, is inescapably

---

[47] Vandermeer, *The Ecology of Agroecosystems*, 19.
[48] See Wezel et al., "Agroecology as a Science, a Movement and a Practice."
[49] A classic treatment of this topic is Freire, *¿Extensión o comunicación?*

value-laden and goal-directed.[50] While science certainly contributes to the realization of agroecology's normative vision, it is neither the only nor the primary contributor. Finally, agroecology challenges these presumptions about science by displaying an integration of science, practice, and politics, showing us how distinct forms of knowledge and ways of knowing need not be mutually exclusive or rivalrous.[51] While this Element focuses especially on agroecological science, we will soon see how an engagement with agroecological science cannot ultimately be separated from agroecological practice and politics.

In this regard, some agroecologists helpfully characterize agroecology as a "dialogue of wisdoms" (*diálogo de saberes*), a phrase that highlights horizontal encounters between scientists, practitioners, activists, and other contributors, demonstrating how their respective "wisdoms" can be coherently integrated.[52] The phrase is significant, suggesting that agroecology does not simply receive wisdom from the participants in the dialogue but is itself a kind of wisdom tradition. This contrasts with Russell Hittinger's observation that the modern West lacks wisdom traditions, which he believes complicates the dialogue about natural law between social teaching and Western secularism. Hittinger writes that "a wisdom tradition is open to reality as a whole," embodying a "natural transcendence," whereas "the modern, Western mind does not view nature or the 'natural' as 'impregnated with immanent wisdom.'"[53] In contrast to this view, contributors to agroecology come from diverse backgrounds – West and East, North and South – and they participate in a discipline characterized precisely by an openness to reality and the discovery of wisdom in the created world. This openness to reality, I argue, is what makes Catholic social teaching's engagement with agroecology especially generative. With this in mind, it is to a closer consideration of this engagement that we now turn.

---

[50] For more on values in science, see Douglas, *Science, Policy, and the Value-Free Ideal*. For more on values in agroecology, see Lacey, *Values and Objectivity in Science*.

[51] Consider Aristotle's distinctions between *epistēmē* (scientific knowledge that is universal, invariable, and context-independent), *technē* (knowledge that is pragmatic, variable, context-dependent, and tied broadly to crafts and technical knowledge that produce artifacts), and *phronesis* (practical wisdom related to deliberation about praxis or action, which is also pragmatic, variable, and context-dependent). Drawing on the work of Bent Flyvbjerg, Emilio Travieso persuasively argues that these forms of rationality roughly correspond to agroecology as a science, practice, and politics, respectively. They are not mutually exclusive and can be coherently integrated, as agroecology attempts to do. Travieso, "Agroecology, Aristotle, and Value(s)." See Flyvbjerg, *Making Social Science Matter*.

[52] Altieri, "Linking Ecologists and Traditional Farmers in the Search for Sustainable Agriculture," 36; Martínez-Torres and Rosset, "*Diálogo de Saberes* in La Vía Campesina."

[53] Hittinger, "The Situation of Natural Law in Catholic Theology," 119–120, quoting the ITC's *In Search of a Universal Ethic*.

2 A Tilling That Keeps

Introduction

The previous section introduced agroecology as an approach to agriculture that both tills and keeps the world, indicating its resonances with the natural law ethic found in Catholic social teaching. That ethic encourages us to provide for ourselves and for one another while also preserving the sources that make such provisioning possible. Agroecology offers practical tools to do just that by patterning agriculture on ecology rather than industry.

This section focuses on the ecological rationale that underpins agroecology, exploring its implications for Catholic social teaching's natural law ethic and the development of an ecology capable of remedying the damage we have done to our common home. How does agroecology conceptualize this ecological rationale derived from the nature of agroecosystems and the ecological principles and processes that govern them? How do agroecologists implement this rationale in practice? How does this implementation promote mitigation and adaptation in response to climate change? What is the broader significance of this ecological rationale for the social teaching tradition? These are the central questions this section seeks to address.

Industrial Agriculture

Earlier we saw Altieri characterize agroecology as an attempt "to reinstate a more ecological rationale into agricultural production," contrasting it with industrial agriculture's industrial ideal. We also noted that agroecological science began as a movement critical of industrializing trends in agricultural science. Therefore, to understand agroecology and its stakes, it is helpful to first examine industrial agriculture and consider agroecology's critique.[54]

Industrial agriculture emerged in the nineteenth century with the Industrial Revolution.[55] As a form of agriculture, it is not unique in its damage to humans and other creatures. Writing in the fourth century, Ambrose of Milan begins *On Naboth*, a treatise describing brutal labor practices among landowners of northern Italy, with the following words: "The story of Naboth is an old one, but it is repeated every day." Drawing on the scriptural account of King Ahab's land grab from Naboth, a small farmer, and Ahab's arrangement of his subsequent murder (1 Kgs 21), Ambrose critiques an avaricious agriculture that uses and abuses people, practices that long predate industrial agriculture.[56] Agricultural

---

[54] For a defense of industrial agriculture, see Avery, *Saving the World with Pesticides and Plastics*.
[55] Mazoyer and Roudart, *A History of World Agriculture*, 313–353.
[56] Ambrose of Milan, "On Naboth," sec. 1.1; Brown, *Through the Eye of a Needle*, 138–147.

history not only offers countless instances of similar use and abuse, it is also replete with examples of exploitation and degradation of soils and the wider creaturely world – an exploitation and degradation so pervasive across the centuries that the agroecologist Wes Jackson calls it the problem *of* agriculture, in contrast to problems *in* agriculture.[57] Industrial agriculture does not break from these pathologies but continues and exacerbates them. Certainly, its story is one of extraordinary advances in agricultural productivity, which have indelibly shaped the world as we know it. But its story has also been one of profound social and ecological upheaval.

The establishment of industrial agriculture depended on as it also consolidated an ongoing revolution in forms of land tenure that had organized human life for centuries. Enforcement of owners' exclusive right to property and land enclosure furthered the dispossessions of countless commoners, indigenous peoples, and others who previously had rights to access and use land.[58] Since the nineteenth century, the rural exodus throughout the world and a vast demographic shift to urban centers are phenomena closely associated with the advance of industrial agriculture.[59]

As already indicated, agroecologists often link industrial agriculture to exploitative and degrading treatment of agricultural workers, as well as to inequalities in the concentration of land and power within the agri-food system.[60] "That system is also rife with other injustices, such as the maldistribution of the food it produces and the fact that approximately a third of all food is wasted."[61] Between 713 and 757 million people experience hunger, and approximately 2.3 billion are moderately or severely food insecure.[62] Significantly, the vast majority of the hungry and food insecure are smallholder farmers, agricultural workers, herders, and indigenous peoples who live in rural areas.[63] The reasons for this are complex and varied but include the fact that affected communities usually face difficulty in accessing or

---

[57] Jackson, *New Roots for Agriculture*, 1–4.
[58] Mazoyer and Roudart, *A History of World Agriculture*, 314–315, 332–351, 467–468; Neeson, *Commoners*; Whelan, *Blood in the Fields*, 42–65.
[59] According to one study, in 1800, approximately 90 percent of the world's population lived in rural settings. Today, over half of the world's population lives in urban areas. See Ritchie and Roser, "Urbanization."
[60] Shiva, *The Violence of the Green Revolution*; Thompson and Wiggins, *The Human Cost of Food*; Hendrickson et al., "The Food System."
[61] United Nations Environment Programme, "Food Waste Index Report 2024," 2. Ritchie, *Not the End of the World*, 144–192.
[62] Food and Agricultural Organization et al., *The State of Food Security and Nutrition in the World 2024*.
[63] This claim, along with the rest of the paragraph, draws on Mazoyer and Roudart, *A History of World Agriculture*, 9–10; Schutter, "Access to Land and the Right to Food"; UN Millennium Project, "Halving Hunger," 4–6.

securing adequate land to farm, especially given the increasing pressure from industrial agriculture and other forms of extractivism. The land to which affected communities do have access is often marginal for agriculture: arid, hilly, and rain-fed. Relatedly, because of the excessive production associated with industrial agriculture and an international trading regime pitting rich and poor farmers in competition with one another, the prices affected communities receive for their products typically cannot guarantee an adequate living for themselves or their families.

Besides industrial agriculture's effects on social life, agroecologists also point to its damage to the wider creaturely world. In *Silent Spring,* Carson documents that damage in relation to indiscriminate pesticide and agrochemical usage. Indeed, the cost of industrial agriculture to creaturely life has been immense, leading to widespread pollution of the kind described by Carson, as well as to the degradation and destruction of habitat, and the overexploitation of forests, fisheries, and soils.[64] In recent years, the Intergovernmental Panel on Climate Change (IPCC) has emphasized the extent to which the agri-food system is a major driver of climate change, estimating its contribution at between 21 percent and 37 percent of total anthropogenic emissions of greenhouse gases worldwide.[65]

But what is industrial agriculture and how is it practiced? As its name implies, this agriculture models crop and livestock production primarily on industry. In her study of its development in the United States, Fitzgerald refers to the rise of "an industrial logic," according to which "every farm a factory" became the normative ideal for agriculture.[66] Indeed, many of the interrelated practices associated with industrial agriculture in our own day – large-scale intensive tillage, monoculture, mechanization, reliance on inorganic fertilizer and chemical pest control, genetic manipulation of plants and animals, irrigation, and confined animal feeding operations (CAFOs) – derive directly from industry, often giving fields and livestock operations the appearance of factories.[67]

All agriculture involves intentional cultivation (*cultura*) of land (*agri*) for human purposes, resulting in a biological simplification of the landscape as humans promote certain uses of it and inhibit others. However, in its overriding focus on the maximization of production of a target crop, industrial agriculture's

---

[64] United Nations Environment Programme, "Assessing the Environmental Impacts of Consumption and Production."
[65] Intergovernmental Panel on Climate Change, *Climate Change and Land*, 8.
[66] See Fitzgerald, *Every Farm a Factory*. For related studies, see also Carson, *Silent Spring*; Scott, *Seeing Like a State*, 262–306; Henke, *Cultivating Science, Harvesting Power*.
[67] According to Altieri, in mechanization, monoculture, and standardization, certain forms of organic agriculture mimic industrial agriculture. However, they forego synthetic chemical inputs and certain prohibited substances, substituting other inputs instead, which Altieri refers to as "input substitution." Altieri, *Agroecology*, ix; Rosset and Altieri, "Agroecology versus Input Substitution."

simplification is especially radical.[68] Prior to cultivation, the land's existing flora and fauna must be cleared. During cultivation, chemical fertilizers are employed to maximize the harvestable yield of the target crop. Additional plants that appear are considered "weeds" and eliminated by herbicides. Pesticides prevent insect herbivores – "pests" – from eating the crop. The purpose of applying fertilizers, herbicides, and pesticides is primarily to increase production, supplying the target crop with nutrients while eliminating competing plants or insects. Notably, the industrial ideal simplifies and reshapes not only the creaturely world but also the very language we use to describe it. For example, terms like "weed" and "pest" are not precise taxonomic classifications but rather imply a particular hermeneutic of creation, its creatures, and their use.[69]

An axiomatic agroecological conviction is that farms are not factories and should not be treated as such. As Goodman, Sorj, and Wilkinson explain, agriculture confronts industry "*with a natural production process.*" Historically, in contrast to other areas of economic life, agriculture could not easily be transformed into an industrial process, because there is "no industrial alternative to the biological transformation of solar energy into food."[70] Yet, industrial agriculture attempts to do just that, steadily replacing agriculture's traditional reliance on biology and ecology with purchased inputs. Hence, in industrial agriculture, pesticides, herbicides, and fungicides are used to address problem insects, plants, and pathogens, replacing biological and other forms of control.[71] Chemical fertilizers meet the nutritional needs of crops, replacing renewable sources of fertility that rely on biomass and nutrient cycling. Genetic manipulation of seeds replaces natural processes of plant evolution, selection, and adaptation.[72] All these replacements represent the industrial transformation of biological and ecological realities. They are part of a systematic attempt to resist, minimize, and even eliminate the dynamism and unpredictability of the wider creaturely world as a force beyond human power and control.[73]

While certain natural constraints have traditionally governed where, what, and when it is possible to cultivate agriculturally,[74] the logic of industrial agriculture has resisted these constraints. Its modus operandi has been to engage and reshape the creaturely world to maximize the production of harvestable

---

[68] The notion of radical simplification comes from Scott, *Seeing Like a State*, 262–263.
[69] Vandermeer, *The Ecology of Agroecosystems*, 218.
[70] Goodman, Sorj, and Wilkinson, *From Farming to Biotechnology*, 1, emphasis in original.
[71] See Whelan, "Agroecology, Biological Control, and Catholic Social Teaching."
[72] Altieri, *Agroecology*, 55–62.
[73] Goodman, Sorj, and Wilkinson, *From Farming to Biotechnology*, 1–3; Scott, *Seeing Like a State*, 262–306.
[74] Federico, *Feeding the World*, 5–15.

Christianity and Agroecology 19

crops. One consequence of this productivist focus, as already noted, is the radical simplification of the agricultural landscape, evidenced by the uniformity of much agriculture today and its extensive fields of genetically identical varieties.[75]

This radical simplification has also reshaped the world and its creatures to meet the demands of industry. Plant breeding of crops like corn exemplifies this industrial agricultural logic at work. In the early twentieth century, the genetic variability of traditional open-pollinated varieties posed a problem for agricultural industrialization due to the diversity of the plants, which was an obstacle to mechanization. Corn ears ripened at different rates and heights, and the plants were often susceptible to lodging, which is the bending over of stems. In response, scientists developed hybrid varieties that resisted lodging and ripened at uniform rates and heights, making them mechanizable. R.E. Webb and W.M. Bruce, two proponents of such phytoengineering, distilled this industrial agricultural logic of reshaping the creaturely world to fit the demands of industry: "Machines are not made to harvest crops; in reality, crops must be designed to be harvested by machines."[76]

Pope Francis's account of the technocratic paradigm in *Laudato si'* provides a good description of how industrial agriculture and its supporting science often operate in practice. It is a paradigm in which the scientist or farmer subject wields knowledge and technology to gain power over creaturely objects, and in which the scientific and experimental method becomes a technique of control. "It is as if the subject were to find itself in the presence of something formless, completely open to manipulation," Francis observes, "extract[ing] everything possible" from creatures, "frequently ignoring or forgetting the reality" before them (no. 106).[77] If the creaturely world is a book, it is as if the pages are basically blank, to be written on as we wish.

From the vantage of agroecology, then, industrial agriculture disregards the complexities of the created world and runs against its grain. One consequence is damage to creaturely life, including the sources that sustain industrial agriculture's own ongoing productivity.[78] Hence, industrial agriculture's intensive tillage and mechanization erode and degrade soil. Its irrigation systems overdraw and deplete water, and its fertilizer and chemical runoff pollute it. Those

---

[75] Khoury et al., "Crop Genetic Erosion"; Curry, "Breeding Uniformity and Banking Diversity."
[76] Kloppenburg, *First the Seed*. 126.
[77] See also ITC, *In Search of a Universal Ethic*, sec. 3.3.72.
[78] For the claims of this paragraph, see Millennium Ecosystem Assessment, *Ecosystems and Human Well-Being*; Rockström et al., "A Safe Operating Space for Humanity"; Campbell et al., "Agriculture Production as a Major Driver of the Earth System Exceeding Planetary Boundaries"; Balmford et al., "The Environmental Costs and Benefits of High-Yield Farming"; Kremen and Miles, "Ecosystem Services in Biologically Diversified versus Conventional Farming Systems."

directly involved in agricultural labor often experience high levels of pesticide and agrochemical exposure. Even those of us at a remove from agricultural production ingest such substances in the water we drink, the food we eat, and the air we breathe. Similarly, almost every aspect of industrial agriculture depends on non-renewable fossil fuels, exacerbating climate change: the clearing of forests and other vegetation to plant crops, the fabrication of agrochemicals, the reliance on tractors and mechanization, and the processing and distribution of food and other agricultural products.[79]

Even our brief consideration of agroecology's critique has shown us that industrial agriculture is not simply a scientific and technical operation, the straightforward raising of crops and livestock to meet human needs. Industrial agriculture – like all agriculture – also presents us with a hermeneutic of creation. When we closely attend to industrial agriculture, we encounter certain assumptions about the nature of the world (cosmology), as well as the human creature (anthropology) and our role on the earth (ethics). For industrial agriculture, it is as if the world is like a blank page. Humans are the principal authors, writing their scientific and technical mastery onto the landscape. And industrial agriculture's primary ethical standard is the maximization of production for humans, even if it comes at the cost of creaturely life.

Of course, industrial agriculture's hermeneutic of creation is not the only one available to us. We can similarly ask about agroecology's. Let us now delve further into its approach to a tilling that also keeps.

Agroecology's Ecological Grammar

As we have just seen, industrial agriculture's primary goal is the maximization of production, reflecting a belief in productionism – the notion that production is the sole norm for the moral evaluation of agriculture.[80] Accordingly, the main argument employed by industrial agricultural advocates against agroecology is that it is unproductive and incapable of feeding the world. Nobel Prize–winning economist Amartya Sen acknowledges the "mesmerizing simplicity" of this focus on production.[81] However, given what we discussed earlier – that the world already produces more than enough food to feed everyone and that so much of what is produced is wasted – the persistence of hunger is clearly more than a problem of production alone, and its alleviation requires addressing the maldistribution and waste of what is already produced.

Agroecology also values production but differs from industrial agriculture in its approach. Despite the fact that agroecology has received far less institutional

---

[79] See Intergovernmental Panel on Climate Change, *Climate Change and Land*.
[80] Thompson, *The Spirit of Soil*, 47–71.   [81] Sen, *Poverty and Famines*, 7–8.

and financial support from governments, research centers, and other organizations than industrial agriculture, agroecologically managed farms – both small- and large-scale – can be as productive as industrially managed ones.[82] One crucial difference between agroecology and industrial agriculture lies not in the importance of production but in whether production should be the sole ethical norm for agriculture. Additionally, agroecology and industrial agriculture also diverge on how best to preserve production across time, how to feed people without degrading the sources that sustain production, and how to address the inequalities and injustices within the existing agri-food system.

Productionism easily obscures how the provisioning of harvestable products is embedded within manifold processes foundational to life on this planet. These processes include primary production, soil formation and fertility, biomass and nutrient cycling, and pollination.[83] They are vital not only to an agroecosystem's ability to produce at all but also to other processes that regulate or moderate climate, soil, water, and air quality. Together, all of these processes enable and support creaturely life.[84] Advocates of industrial agriculture often articulate a tradeoff between maximizing production and preserving such ecosystemic processes.[85] By contrast, agroecologists contend that it is possible to provide for ourselves and for one another by better understanding, preserving, and harnessing these ecosystemic processes – working with rather than against their grain.[86] In short, agroecologists believe it is possible both to till and keep the world.

In this way, agroecology seeks to reinstate what Altieri calls an ecological rationale into agriculture, patterning production on ecology rather than industry. Agroecologists describe this ecological rationale in different ways. Altieri, as we saw earlier, appeals to the nature of agroecosystems and the principles and processes by which they function, while other agroecologists speak of "the complex and diverse rules of ecology"[87] or "the fundamental natural laws of ecosystems" as the primary guides for agricultural practice, planning, and management.[88]

---

[82] See the case studies in Montgomery, *Growing a Revolution*.
[83] This paragraph draws on Millennium Ecosystem Assessment, *Ecosystems and Human Well-Being*.
[84] Millennium Ecosystem Assessment, *Ecosystems and Human Well-Being*.
[85] This position is sometimes called 'land sparing' because it regards provisioning as inherently degradative and so maximizes yields on certain areas in order to spare land for conservation on others. See Phalan et al., "How Can Higher-Yield Farming Help to Spare Nature?"
[86] Perfecto and Vandermeer, "The Agroecological Matrix as Alternative to the Land-Sparing /Agriculture Intensification Model."
[87] Carroll, Vandermeer, and Rosset, *Agroecology*, x.
[88] Vandermeer and Perfecto, *Ecological Complexity and Agroecology*, 1. See also Gliessman et al., *Agroecology*, 1. For the formulation of agroecological principles, see High Level Panel of

We can refer to these appeals by agroecologists to principles, rules, and laws as an ecological grammar, analogous to the grammar governing a natural language. Just as languages have principles, rules, and laws that order their use, the notion of an ecological grammar suggests natural ecosystems do too. A central agroecological goal is to discern this grammar and imitate it agriculturally.

Once again, Francis's descriptions in *Laudato si'* are helpful for understanding what is at stake. Whereas industrial agriculture and its supporting science endeavor to extend human control over creaturely objects, treating them as formless and open to manipulation, agroecology's ecological grammar, by contrast, attunes us to "the possibilities offered by the things themselves," the reception of "what nature itself allows, as if from its own hand" (no. 106). Put differently, for agroecology, the creaturely world is not a blank page for us to write on as we wish. Rather, if the creaturely world is a book, we are not its authors, and there is writing already discernable on its pages, to which we must learn to attend and respond agriculturally.

Agricultural Biodiversification

Fostering biodiversification within agroecosystems is essential to how agroecology respects and works with this ecological grammar.[89] Besides being an agroecological principle itself, biodiversification is foundational to other agroecological principles. The implementation of principles like the preferential use of local renewable sources, closure of nutrient and biomass cycles, reduction of dependence on purchased inputs, promotion of soil health and functioning, and enhancement of beneficial synergisms within the agroecosystem[90] all depend on and lead to biodiversification, just as biodiversification depends on and leads to them.

Taken together, the purpose of these and other agroecological principles is to make agriculture less like a linear, industrial process, in which sources are degraded and by-products become waste, and more like a circular, ecosystemic process, in which sources are preserved and by-products are reused. Achieving

---

Experts on Food Security and Nutrition, "Agroecological and Other Innovative Approaches," 39–42; Wezel et al., "Agroecological Principles and Elements and Their Implications for Transitioning to Sustainable Food Systems."

[89] It is helpful to distinguish between the collection of plants and animals that farmers cultivate, typically referred to as "agrobiodiversity" or "planned" biodiversity, and the biodiversity that spontaneously arrives in the agroecosystem or its environs, typically called "associated" or "wild" biodiversity. Both kinds of biodiversity are central to agroecology. Perfecto, Vandermeer, and Wright, *Nature's Matrix*, 18–19.

[90] These are agroecological principles formulated by the High Level Panel of Experts on Food Security and Nutrition, "Agroecological and Other Innovative Approaches," 39–42.

this requires agroecosystemic biodiversification. To that end, agroecologists point to practices like polyculture (growing multiple crops simultaneously), mixed cultivation (raising crops, along with livestock or fisheries together), agroforestry (the simultaneous cultivation of both trees and agricultural crops), managing hedgerows and buffer vegetation around perimeters or pathways, crop rotations (planting different crops in specific, recurring sequences), fallowing, reducing or minimizing soil tillage, and integrating high quantities of organic matter into the soil (through composting, incorporating crop residues, among other methods).[91]

Gliessman contends the "central priority" of agroecological management "is creating a more complex, diverse agroecosystem, because only with high diversity is there a potential for beneficial interactions."[92] Gliessman uses the term "complex" (from the Greek *com* "with, together" and *plectere* "to weave, braid, twine, entwine") in a specific sense: to name the interwovenness of the various creaturely members of ecological communities and how new characteristics emerge from this interwovenness that are irreducible to analysis or aggregation of the parts. Such irreducibility derives from the fact that parts acquire new characteristics as a consequence of the interwovenness, which then changes the whole, which in turn changes the parts, and so on. Crucial to the notion of complexity is the ongoing transformative relationship between parts and wholes.[93]

Biodiversification helps establish synergies between creatures and processes within the agroecosystem that then redound to the good of this whole. A practical presumption of industrial agricultural monoculture is that plants compete with one another, which is why any plant apart from the target crop(s) is called a "weed" and then eliminated.[94] However, plants, like other creatures, do not just compete for available resources; they can also cooperate.[95] An especially ancient and enduring example of how biodiversification fosters these beneficial and cooperative interactions is the *milpa* agricultural system. *Milpa* is a word that comes from the Nahuatl *mil-pa* for "a cultivated field," and it is an approach to intercropping maize,[96] beans, and squash that indigenous peoples throughout North and Central America developed and adapted – and that continues to be practiced by many smallholders today. Among some

---

[91] Altieri, *Agroecology*; Gliessman et al., *Agroecology*.   [92] Gliessman et al., *Agroecology*, 184.
[93] See Vandermeer and Perfecto, *Ecological Complexity and Agroecology*, 1–7.
[94] Shiva, *Who Really Feeds the World?* 6–7.
[95] Garibaldi et al., "Complementarity and Synergisms among Ecosystem Services Supporting Crop Yield."
[96] Fussell, "Translating Maize into Corn."

peoples, it is referred to as "the Three Sisters," a reference to the bond uniting the three crops on which the system is based.[97]

The *milpa* has endured because of the benefits from growing these crops in polyculture. Among those benefits, the structure of the maize plant provides support for the beans and enables them to grow above the ground, where they would otherwise be more susceptible to pests and plant disease. The squash covers and protects the soil, retains moisture, and suppresses weeds. The beans are legumes – from the plant family *Fabaceae*, which also includes peas, soybeans, alfalfa, and clovers. The symbiotic relationship legumes have with rhizobia bacteria enables them to convert atmospheric nitrogen into usable forms for the maize and squash. There are also important nutritional benefits to *milpa* agriculture, a system developed to meet people's basic energy and protein requirements.[98]

In general, the *milpa*, like other polycultures, tends to have fewer problems with insect herbivores than monocultures because polycultures provide more habitat for natural enemies. Polycultures are also more efficient at capturing light, water, and other nutrients, because creatures occupy diverse spatial and temporal niches within the agroecosystem and play different roles.[99] In summary, the complementarities of polycultures like *milpas* are multiple and complex. As a result, the *milpa*, like diverse, integrated agroecosystems more generally, are not only resilient but can also be highly productive – much more so than if you plant each crop alone.[100]

A Diverse and Permanent Agriculture

Stephen Gliessman explains the underlying premise of much agroecology: "The greater the ... similarity of an agroecosystem to the natural ecosystems in the biogeographic region, the greater the likelihood that the agroecosystem will be sustainable."[101] Given this, agroecologically managed agroecosystems vary considerably in accordance with local ecological conditions.[102] As we will see next, there are examples of systems patterned on prairies. But there are also systems patterned on deserts,[103] tropical forests,[104] temperate deciduous forests,[105] and other types of ecosystems.

---

[97] See Kimmerer, *Braiding Sweetgrass*, 128–140.
[98] Mt. Pleasant, "Food Yields and Nutrient Analyses of the Three Sisters."
[99] Vandermeer et al., "Global Change and Multi-Species Agroecosystems," 6–9.
[100] Fonteyne et al., "Review of Agronomic Research on the *Milpa*, the Traditional Polyculture System of Mesoamerica."
[101] Gliessman et al., *Agroecology*, 288.
[102] Reijntjes, Haverkort, and Waters-Bayer, *Farming for the Future*, 58–60.
[103] Nabhan, *The Desert Smells Like Rain*; Nabhan, *Gathering the Desert*.
[104] Toledo et al., "The Multiple Use of Tropical Forests by Indigenous Peoples in Mexico."
[105] Smith, *Tree Crops*.

Unlike the radical simplicity of industrial agroecosystems, natural ecosystems tend to be more biodiverse.[106] Consider my local ecosystem in central Texas, known as the Blackland Prairie, which was historically dominated by tallgrass prairies on uplands and decidous forests along rivers and creeks. Before these lands were plowed and planted by settlers in the nineteenth century, the Wacoan indigenous peoples lived here, subsisting by hunting, fishing, and practicing *milpa* agriculture.[107] The prairies supported mixes of tall-growing perennial grasses like big and little bluestem, Indiangrass, and switchgrass; bluebonnets and other native wildflowers; and large fauna like plains bison, elk, pronghorns, bears, and wolves, in addition to smaller creatures and countless other organisms. Since the late nineteenth century, agricultural production of a handful of dominant monocultural systems of annuals like cotton, corn, and wheat, along with cattle raising and the growth of human settlements, has radically simplified and transformed this ecology.[108]

A prominent example of the agroecological approach of imitating natural ecosystems like the prairie is the work of the Land Institute in Salina, Kansas.[109] Unlike prairie grasses, which are perennials and so live for two or more years, most agricultural crops are annuals and so live for a single growing season. Because of their short lifespan, annuals must be replanted continually, which often means plowing and leaving the soil exposed and hence susceptible to erosion, as well as applying herbicide to suppress vegetation competing with the target crop. The Land Institute is therefore developing novel perennial grain and seed varieties[110] – a breeding program that essentially pursues direct

---

[106] Species variety is only one kind of diversity. Ecosystems and their creatures are also genetically diverse, which refers to the variety of inherited traits within and among species, such as prairie grasses like big bluestem or animals like the plains bison. Ecosystems are also diverse structurally in terms of the different creatures present and the feeding or trophic relationships between producers, herbivores, predators, and parasites. There are also diverse functional processes within ecosystems, such as productivity, nutrient cycling, and pollination. Finally, ecosystems have diverse spatial arrangements among members, such as distinct root systems of prairie grasses or canopy levels of a forest. See Gliessman et al., *Agroecology*, 183–201.

[107] Barker, "Thomas M. Duke to Stephen F. Austin, 06-Xx-1824," Part 1, 842–843.

[108] Chapman and Boen, *The Natural History of Texas*, 58–70.

[109] My account of the Land Institute is based on Jackson, *New Roots for Agriculture*. See also the Land Institute's website, which has a wealth of scientific papers and other information (https://landinstitute.org/). The Land Institute calls its approach "natural systems" or "perennial" agriculture. It is also agroecological because it envisions an agriculture modeled on the ecological principles and processes operative in prairie ecosystems to achieve ecological goods like preventing erosion, regenerating soil, and managing insect herbivores.

[110] Much of the Land Institute's work is still in the research phase. The domesticated perennial grain Kernza, which originated from a wheatgrass variety (*Thinopyrum intermedium*), is an exception. Kernza is grown by farmers and even being brewed into beer through a partnership with Patagonia. See www.patagoniaprovisions.com/pages/why-beer.

domestication of wild plants and hybridization of existing annual varieties with their wild relatives.[111] Because the sorghum, wheat, rice, oilseed, and legume varieties bred by the Land Institute are perennials, they do not require frequent replanting and do not leave soil exposed. Perennials also have deep and elaborate root systems that hold the soil in place, further preventing erosion, and that build soil and store carbon through the accumulation of organic matter.

In addition to breeding novel perennial grain and seed varieties, the Land Institute also seeks to integrate them into polycultures. As noted earlier, integrating legumes into an agroecosystem brings benefits because of their symbiotic relationship with rhizobia bacteria. Legumes convert atmospheric nitrogen into usable forms, which can decrease or eliminate reliance on synthetic nitrogen fertilizer. Another benefit of biodiverse cropping systems like those of the Land Institute is that they provide excellent habitat for natural enemies of insect herbivores, as well as for bees, butterflies, birds, and other creatures that participate in ecological processes like pollination.

While agroecology names, to paraphrase Aristotle, the agricultural art that imitates nature,[112] an example like the Land Institute shows that imitation is more complex than might appear at first glance. Imitating nature is distinct from copying or plagiarizing it[113] – or even from restoring it.[114] Art is not nature, so an agriculture patterned on the prairie differs – sometimes significantly – from any particular prairie.[115] The Land Institute's agricultural art does not reproduce wild prairie grasses or otherwise aim at verisimilitude. Instead, that art involves discerning the ecological principles underlying the prairie, such as biodiversity and perenniality, along with how these principles foster agriculturally beneficial processes that prevent erosion, regenerate soil, and control insect herbivore populations, among other benefits. Based on this discernment, the Land Institute has bred novel perennial grain and seed varieties adapted to polycultures that

---

[111] Farmers have used direct domestication for millennia to adapt wild plants and animals for human use. This process involves identifying desirable wild plant species (for instance, varieties that retain seeds until harvest or that mature uniformly), collecting the seeds, and re-planting them. Hybridization involves combining desirable genes found in two or more different varieties to produce a new variety that is superior in certain respects to the previous ones. In contrast to both these methods, genetic modification of organisms (GMOs) involves inserting DNA into plant cells. Consequently, while direct domestication and hybridization operate on whole organisms, the new genetic technologies operate at the cellular and molecular levels. The former two techniques rely on sexual reproduction to transfer genetic material, whereas GMOs circumvent this process, manipulating and moving genes between organisms. None of the perennial grain and seed varieties being developed by the Land Institute are GMOs. See Crews and Cattani, "Strategies, Advances, and Challenges in Breeding Perennial Grain Crops"; Kloppenburg, *First the Seed*.

[112] Aristotle, *Physics*, 199a.

[113] Berry, *The Poetry of William Carlos Williams of Rutherford*, 153–155.

[114] Higgs, *Nature by Design*.

[115] Whelan, "Imagination, Agriculture, and the Plagiarization of Nature."

reproduce – within agroecosystems themselves – the kinds of ecological principles and processes we find at work in prairies.

Mitigation and Adaption

We have been examining agroecology as an approach to agriculture that is both productive and preserves the sources of its own productivity. Agroecology accomplishes this by relying on an ecological grammar derived from the nature of agroecosystems and the principles and processes by which they function. Instead of reshaping the locale to fit agriculture, agroecology reshapes agriculture to fit the locale, patterning agriculture on ecology rather than industry. Central to this grammar is biodiversification, which enables agroecosystems to function more like natural ecosystems than factories. By working with the ecological principles and processes that sustain creaturely life, agroecology establishes beneficial interactions that contribute to the good of the whole agroecosystem, such as retaining soil and preventing erosion, building soil fertility, and biologically controlling potentially problematic insect herbivores.

Another associated benefit that comes from working with ecological principles and processes is the potential for agroecology to mitigate climate change through reductions in carbon emissions. While modern industrial agriculture depends heavily on fossil fuels in every aspect of its operation, agroecology seeks to minimize such dependence. Instead of using purchased inputs for fertility, agroecology relies on renewable sources and ecological processes, closing nutrient and biomass cycles, and building soil health and biological activity by intercropping legumes and adding organic matter.[116] Instead of using industrially derived inputs to eliminate problematic insects, agroecology manages them through biological control, which mimics predator–prey dynamics in natural ecosystems. Agroecology also mitigates climate change by implementing practices that sequester atmospheric carbon in trees, crops, and soils, such as preventing deforestation, reducing or even eliminating tillage, integrating cover crops, retaining in-field crop residue, and generally fostering agroecosystemic biodiversification.[117]

Besides mitigation, another benefit agroecology brings is the potential to increase the adaptive capacity of agroecosystems in the face of changing, unpredictable, and increasingly extreme climatic conditions.[118] While industrial agriculture is characterized by radical simplicity and dependence on

---

[116] Montgomery, *Growing a Revolution*.
[117] Intergovernmental Panel on Climate Change, *Climate Change and Land*; Benkeblia, *Climate Change and Crop Production*, 105–130.
[118] Altieri, *Agroecology*, x; Gliessman et al., *Agroecology*, 217–236, 379–388; Intergovernmental Panel on Climate Change, *Climate Change and Land*.

external inputs, making it highly vulnerable to failure,[119] agroecology contends that biodiverse agroecosystems are crucial for fostering adaptation and resilience.[120] In ecological science, resilience is a term of art referring to an ecosystem's ability to absorb variability and disturbance while still persisting across time. However, in agroecology, while resilience can certainly include persistence – such as the capacity of an agroecosystem to absorb and recover from variability and disturbance – it can also include the capacity of agroecosystems to transform as a consequence of such variability and disturbance, adapting to the new circumstances and entering into a new regime of stability.[121] Resilience is therefore a helpful concept for managing systems like agroecosystems, which are constantly undergoing changes to which managers must prepare for and respond.[122]

Biodiversification is crucial for fostering the adaptive capacity of agroecosystems because the greater an ecosystem's biodiversity, the greater its capacity to absorb and resist stress and disturbance, as well as recover and even reorganize subsequently.[123] An important aspect of an ecosystem's adaptive capacity is what ecologists call functional response diversity. The presence of diverse creatures within the system that respond in different ways to variability and disturbance establishes the conditions for better – and worse – adaptations over time, and hence for persistence of underlying relationships within the ecosystem.[124] Another important aspect of an ecosystem's adaptive capacity is what ecologists call functional group diversity. Creatures occupy diverse spatial and temporal niches, performing distinct roles or functions within them, such as pollinating, fixing atmospheric nitrogen, decomposing organic material, and predating other creatures. Sometimes multiple creatures perform the same role and so are part of the same functional group. Often, there are more

---

[119] Heinemann et al., "Sustainability and Innovation in Staple Crop Production in the US Midwest."

[120] Altieri, *Agroecology*, x, 5, 59–62, 92, 99, 106; Gliessman et al., *Agroecology*, 29–31, 183–201, 235, 252, 300; Lin, "Resilience in Agriculture through Crop Diversification"; Liebman and Schulte, "Enhancing Agroecosystem Performance and Resilience through Increased Diversification of Landscapes and Cropping Systems."

[121] The aim is for a system to either stay within its current stability regime or transition to a new one where its elements can still thrive, albeit in different combinations or at varying levels relative to one another. The primary goal is to avoid system collapse, which results in a shift to an inherently unstable regime.

[122] Holling, "Resilience and Stability of Ecological Systems," 16–19. The work of Robert M. May has shown that more complex systems are not necessarily more stable. See Holling's comments on May's understanding of stability in the pages just cited. See May's comments on Holling in May, *Stability and Complexity in Model Ecosystems*, 213–18.

[123] For a critique of this view, see May, *Stability and Complexity in Model Ecosystems*.

[124] Elmqvist et al., "Response Diversity, Ecosystem Change, and Resilience"; Gonzalez and Loreau, "The Causes and Consequences of Compensatory Dynamics in Ecological Communities."

Christianity and Agroecology

creatures than functions, leading to ecological overlaps. When conditions change, overlaps that might have once appeared redundant can become essential for ensuring ongoing function and adaptation of ecosystems to the new conditions.[125]

In recent years, numerous studies have highlighted the adaptive capacity of agroecosystems in the midst of climatic variability and more frequent extreme weather events. Biodiverse agroecosystems, for instance, often fare better at buffering crops from erratic fluctuations in temperature and precipitation.[126] Agroecosystems that avoid disturbing the soil, grow cover crops, retain crop residues, and practice polyculture report better water infiltration and holding capacity. Excess rain does not pool on the surface or lead to runoff, and periods of relative dryness or drought can be better endured.[127] These biodiverse agroecosystems are also less susceptible to landslide incidence and severity, as well as additional kinds of damage associated with hurricanes and other forms of extreme weather.[128] When Hurricane Mitch – among the most powerful Caribbean storms of the previous century – hit Central America in 1998, farms that implemented agroecological practices retained more topsoil, field moisture, and vegetative cover, and suffered less erosion and economic loss than farms that did not.[129]

Throughout the world today, we find farming communities that have developed biodiverse agroecosystems and variable livelihood strategies in order to reduce vulnerability and increase security in the midst of dynamic, unpredictable, and uncontrollable climatic conditions.[130] In explaining this phenomenon, development scholar Robert Chambers contrasts the ecological rationale underlying such diversification with that of the industrial machine. Unlike a machine, which is often vulnerable to failure in any number of its parts, these livelihood strategies and agroecosystems purposefully integrate diversity and redundancy within them, mimicking natural ecosystems and their ecological grammar. Consequently, if one variety, crop, asset, or activity fails, others are

---

[125] Walker, "Conserving Biological Diversity through Ecosystem Resilience," 748–749.

[126] Lin, "Agroforestry Management as an Adaptive Strategy against Potential Microclimate Extremes in Coffee Agriculture"; Lin, Perfecto, and Vandermeer, "Synergies between Agricultural Intensification and Climate Change Could Create Surprising Vulnerabilities for Crops."

[127] Montgomery, *Growing a Revolution*.

[128] Philpott et al., "A Multi-Scale Assessment of Hurricane Impacts on Agricultural Landscapes Based on Land Use and Topographic Features."

[129] Holt-Giménez, "Measuring Farmers' Agroecological Resistance after Hurricane Mitch in Nicaragua."

[130] Toledo, "The Ecological Rationality of Peasant Production"; Ellis, *Rural Livelihoods and Diversity in Developing Countries*; Tengö and Belfrage, "Local Management Practices for Dealing with Change and Uncertainty"; Koohafkan and Altieri, *Globally Important Agricultural Heritage Systems*.

available.[131] In a warming world and as climatic conditions increasingly become unpredictable and extreme, there is wisdom to be gleaned from this alternate approach and its ecological rationale.

Assessing Agroecology's Ecological Grammar

In light of our consideration of agroecology's ecological grammar and its practical implications, we are now in a better position to step back and examine some salient features of that grammar as they bear on the larger argument of this Element. The first is that grammar's convergence with Catholic social teaching's account of natural law, particularly the conviction that by attending to the creaturely world we can discover principles needed to till and keep it, as well as ends and criteria for its wise use. The next section examines this conviction from the vantage point of social teaching. What do we make of it from the vantage point of agroecology?

The first thing to notice is that agroecology's ecological grammar operates both descriptively and normatively. In one sense, that grammar is grounded in the scientific literature under examination here. The agroecological appeal to ecology draws lessons for agricultural practice from empirical observation and scientific study of the world. Crucial to this ecological grammar is that it is discerned and discovered within the world rather than imposed on it. While industrial agriculture regards the world as a blank page, agroecology, in contrast, attends to what is already written, and its practice collaborates with the possibilities offered by things themselves and what the locale permits. Agroecology receives the world as if it possesses a kind of intelligibility and goodness that should be acknowledged, respected, and cooperated with in its use.

At the same time, agroecology's ecological grammar also has normative valences. That grammar is embedded in a form of moral reasoning that is irreducible to science and has affinities to natural law thinking.[132] When biologists speak of something as "good for" an organism or a species, "good" basically means conducive to survival and reproduction, and it does not carry any morally evaluative weight. In contrast, agroecology's appeal to an ecological grammar operates differently and does suggest morally evaluative weight.[133] This is

---

[131] Chambers, *Whose Reality Counts?*, 171.
[132] See Porter, *Natural and Divine Law*, 26, 106; *Nature as Reason*, 123–125; Whelan, "Agroecology's Moral Vision."
[133] Admittedly, agroecologists are not always aware of this normativity and rarely reflect explicitly on it. An exception to this tendency is Wezel et al., "Agroecological Principles and Elements and Their Implications for Transitioning to Sustainable Food Systems," 39–40. For a helpful exploration of these matters with respect to health and disease, see Messer's *Flourishing*, 1–50.

evident in how agroecologists rely on an ecological grammar to evaluate agroecosystems, assessing their relative degradation or ecological integrity, critiquing the industrial patterning of agriculture, and advocating for an alternative. In these ways, agroecology's ecological grammar participates in a form of moral reasoning that has a clear conception of normativity, one that converges with Catholic social teaching's natural law ethic.

Another, related feature of agroecology's ecological grammar is what we might call the limited character of the norms it derives from the wider creaturely world.[134] Agroecology advocates for ecological principles, not recipes, principles that must be embedded and developed within specific contexts.[135] While agroecology discerns a message that it regards as a source of moral insight, that message is not simply read off the surface of things. Rather, it must be discerned, a process that, once again, relates to our being creatures formed within communities. Hence, agroecology and industrial agriculture's divergent hermeneutics of creation. Nor is the message agroecology discerns a static or practically binding moral code. Rather, this natural normativity underdetermines agroecology's own moral commitments, requiring further elaboration through specific practices, virtues, and communal forms. While agroecological principles like biodiversification are generalizable, applying them can include *milpa* agriculture, the perennial polycultures of the Land Institute, or numerous other embodiments, both large- and small-scale. The beliefs, practices, and ways of life of specific communities are what give agroecological principles like biodiversification more determinative form, effectively humanizing and socializing them.

A number of other features of agroecology's ecological grammar relate to the analogy between ecosystems and natural languages. Just as we are "inside" language, we are "inside" ecology as agroecology conceives it, living in ecology as we live in the flesh and depend on other creatures for air, food, drink, clothing, and shelter. Additionally, like languages, ecosystems are both plural and distributed diversely across space and time. As such, languages not only vary geographically, but they also undergo constant change – sometimes even sudden and dramatic change – just as ecosystems do. However, despite such variation and change, languages still have grammars that can guide people into becoming fluent communicators. For instance, Latin has changed so significantly over time that it has become Italian, French, Spanish, Portuguese, and Romanian, but it does not follow that communicating in any of these languages is arbitrary or that at any given moment there is not a grammar that guides their

---

[134] This paragraph draws on Friesen, "Theological Foundations for a Christian Land Ethic."
[135] Nicholls, Altieri, and Vazquez, "Agroecological Principles for the Conversion of Farming Systems," 3–4.

usage. Agroecology's ecological grammar implies something similar regarding ecology. In the analogy between ecosystems and natural languages, we therefore encounter a conception of ecology that – despite ecosystemic diversity, variation, and change – can still meaningfully appeal to discernible principles, rules, and laws to guide tilling and keeping.

Closely related to the foregoing discussion, a final feature of agroecology's ecological grammar crucial to underscore is how it unsettles the idealized ecology still assumed by much ecological theology and ethics today, including by Catholic social teaching. An idealized ecology characteristically excludes the human creature, implying a stark separation between humans and the rest of creation that is in tension with the doctrine of creation. Moreover, as we saw Deane-Drummond observe earlier, idealized ecology tends to invoke stable equilibria, natural balances, and pristine conditions, presenting a picture of ecological relationships that are characterized by harmony and interconnection, without sufficient acknowledgment of ecological dynamism or death.

How does agroecology's ecological grammar differ? We have already seen that it conceives the human creature inside ecology, not outside it. Agroecology inescapably involves human agency, such as we see in the discernment of ecological principles and processes and their agricultural imitation. At the same time, agroecosystems are nature-culture hybrids.[136] Their ecology is shaped as much by changes in land tenure and price fluctuations as by changing climatic conditions, soil degradation, or outbreaks of insect herbivores.[137] The coevolution of ecological and social systems[138] means that the essential sources of an agriculture that tills and keeps are both cultural and natural. Sustaining such an agriculture requires sustaining a people who recognize that how they farm and eat shapes how the world and its creatures are used. Put differently, fostering an agriculture that tills and keeps is more than a technical or scientific problem alone.

Agroecology's ecological grammar differs from an idealized ecology in other ways as well. The aim of agroecological management is to discern an ecological grammar and follow its guidance, which differs from preserving or restoring stable equilibria, natural balances, or pristine ecosystemic conditions. As we saw earlier, agroecology imitates ecology; it does not plagiarize it. What is imitated are the underlying ecological principles and processes – what we might call the creativity animating and ordering the creaturely world – not the surface

---

[136] For an elaboration of this hybridity, see Latour, *We Have Never Been Modern*; Descola, *Beyond Nature and Culture*.
[137] Hecht, "The Evolution of Agroecological Thought," 5.
[138] Northgaard and Sikor, "The Methodology and Practice of Agroecology," 25–39.

visibility of ecosystems.[139] While agroecologists use the language of agroecosystemic balance and integrity, they mean something different by these terms than those who idealize ecology do.[140] For instance, agroecological management seeks to adapt agroecosystems to dynamic, unpredictable, and uncontrollable conditions. While such adaptation can mean an agroecosystem's ability to absorb variability and disturbance and continue to persist, it can also mean an agroecosystem's transformation in the face of such change, along with the development of new relationships within the agroecosystem. Accordingly, whatever integrity or balance characterizes agroecosystems, there are multiple such states and diverse pathways toward achieving them, not just one.[141]

Agroecology's ecological grammar and the reality of ecosystemic dynamism therefore imply no simplistic natural balance or original pristine condition. A good example of this comes from a long-term study of coffee ecosystems in Chiapas, Mexico, in which predator–prey interactions among creatures successfully buffer coffee production against outbreaks of insect herbivores or diseases. Vandermeer, Perfecto, and Philpott, the authors of the study, describe the agroecosystem "not as precisely balanced on the classical engineer's equilibrium point, but more like a spiderweb, achieving structure and resilience from its multiple interconnections" – a structure and resilience arising from multiple nonlinear interactions among creatures that the authors describe as a "higher notion of balance."[142] Significantly, the authors discern this higher balance in a *coffee* agroforestry system – a cash crop that is not indigenous to southern Mexico but came with colonization.[143] Prior to and apart from the development of such coffee agroforestry systems, the Tzeltal and Tzotzil Mayan-descendent peoples of Chiapas had developed the *milpa* and other agroecosystems based on native crops. Yet, coffee is an example of a non-native crop that the Tzeltal and Tzotzil peoples have assimilated into their agriculture and made their own.[144] Simply put, the existence of these and similar agroecosystems troubles appeals to pristine ecological conditions. It

---

[139] Berry, *The Poetry of William Carlos Williams of Rutherford*, 154.

[140] Altieri, *Agroecology*; Gliessman et al., *Agroecology*; Higgs, *Nature by Design*.

[141] Gardner, Ramsden, and Hails, *Agricultural Resilience*. While ecosystems can and do embody states of integrity, balance, or equilibrium, they are always in perpetual motion. Ecosystems can have multiple such states, often visualized by ecologists as valleys separated by ridges. In this analogy, such a state is like a ball at the bottom of a valley. Under certain conditions, the ball might shift to another valley and be unable to return, a phenomenon known as hysteresis (from the Greek *hystérēsis* for "deficiency" or "lagging behind"). The ball might also settle in an unstable state along a ridgeline. New such states are often possible, and none is final. Petraitis, *Multiple Stable States in Natural Ecosystems*, 5, 8, 14, 20, 67.

[142] Vandermeer, Perfecto, and Philpott, "Ecological Complexity and Pest Control in Organic Coffee Production," 528, 536.

[143] Pendergrast, *Uncommon Grounds*, 15–19.

[144] For more on such systems in Chiapas and elsewhere, see Hernández Xoloctozi, *Xolocotzia*.

highlights how, once again, in any given time and place, there are multiple pathways toward achieving the higher notion of balance and integrity that agroecologists are trying to foster within agroecosystems.[145]

Regarding this higher balance and integrity, notice also its occurrence amid predator–prey dynamics and the realities of creaturely death within an agroecosystem. In the example just mentioned, the ant *Azteca instabilis* is a keystone species, driving numerous associated processes of biological control. *Azteca*, along with other ant populations, predates the leaf miner and the coffee bean borer that do damage to coffee. But there are additional interrelationships associated with the formation and spread of *Azteca* ant nests that establish enabling conditions for the survival and increase of natural enemies of other insect herbivores and diseases. In other words, the higher balance making it possible for agroecologists to regulate damage to coffee without recourse to pesticides is an ecological good that is inextricably bound up with the death of certain creatures. In fact, all the ecosystemic processes that agroecologists manage – not just predator–prey dynamics but also soil fertility, nutrient and biomass cycling, and so on – essentially involve the management of creaturely death as constitutive to the existence and ongoing productivity of agroecosystems.

All these features of agroecology's ecological grammar – its relation to a form of reasoning like natural law, its limited character, its analogy to natural languages, and its unsettling of an idealized ecology – have important implications for Catholic social teaching's natural law ethic. We have been examining this ecological grammar through the lens of agroecology. Now, let us consider it in relation to social teaching.

---

[145] Restoration ecologists encounter a similar plurality when seeking to restore degraded ecosystems. At what moment in the past does one look for a reference point? While restoring a painting with an identifiable original condition is one thing, restoring a landscape with an ongoing history is quite another. Additionally, the reality of a warming world and shifting vegetation ranges further complicates the question of what to restore and to what extent historical fidelity should be the guide. Higgs, *Nature by Design*, 38–40.

3 Toward a Deeper Understanding of the Natural Law

Introduction

The previous section examined agroecology as an approach to agriculture that tills and keeps, exploring agroecology's underlying ecological rationale and suggesting its significance for Catholic social teaching's natural law ethic. This section directly addresses and elaborates on that significance, focusing on a limited but critical issue: how agroecology and its ecological rationale can help clarify and deepen social teaching's natural law ethic.

As noted earlier, in recent decades, Catholic social teaching's natural law ethic has ecologized, developing to a point where it now shares significant moral commonalities with agroecology's ecological grammar. Principal among these commonalities is an appeal to ecological principles and processes that offer wisdom and guidance. Both social teaching and agroecology discern an order within the creaturely world that should shape its use. This moral commonality is what makes social teaching's engagement with agroecology especially fruitful. However, there are also crucial differences between social teaching and agroecology. Notably, social teaching's natural law ethic often presumes an idealized ecology characterized by pristine states, static equilibria, and simple harmonies – a conception that overlooks important truths about the creaturely world.

In this section, I argue that agroecology can help Catholic social teaching address this issue, further clarifying and deepening its reflection on the natural law. Agroecology's ecological grammar is more attuned to the realities of the creaturely world we inhabit than the idealized ecology currently embraced by social teaching. It acknowledges ecological dynamism, instability, and creaturely death, while still discerning a moral message within that world to guide its good use. Agroecology's approach therefore offers Catholic social teaching valuable wisdom, and heeding this wisdom can contribute to an ecology capable of remedying the damage we have done to our common home.

"A Grammar That Sets Forth Ends and Criteria for Wise Use"

Before turning to how agroecology can help clarify and deepen Catholic social teaching's natural law ethic, we must first explore the convergences between social teaching and agroecology at greater length. In the previous section, I characterized agroecology as an agricultural art imitative of nature, a discipline whose form of moral reasoning resonates with what the Christian tradition calls the natural law. In the act of imitating nature, as we observed, agroecologists perceive wisdom in the creaturely world. They reason about and reflect on that wisdom by discerning and articulating ecological principles and processes. On these grounds, they distinguish between good and bad approaches to agriculture. In short, this ecological grammar both describes the world and norms its use, guiding the evaluation of the relevant ecological goods and harms of different forms of agriculture, as well as advocacy for an agriculture patterned on ecology rather than industry. Although agroecology does not use the language of natural law and although agroecologists themselves do not frequently reflect explicitly on their form of moral reasoning, agroecology nevertheless presumes a kind of natural law ethic.

Accordingly, there are clear convergences between agroecology and Catholic social teaching related to the natural law that must be acknowledged. Like agroecology, social teaching approaches the wider creaturely world as an order that sustains our lives, consisting of ecological principles and processes we did not create, which possess intrinsic goodness, intelligibility, and integrity, and can guide moral action. We can discern these principles and processes, just as we can also interiorize, articulate, reflect on, debate, and revise them. In a word, agroecology and social teaching's natural law ethic share the conviction that the creaturely world has a reality and purpose apart from humankind, and that it bears a message that should shape our use of it.

Pope Benedict XVI gives clear voice to Catholic social teaching's natural law ethic in his encyclical *Caritas in veritate* (2008) in a passage already referenced earlier but worth quoting at length:

> The environment is God's gift to everyone, and in our use of it we have a responsibility towards the poor, towards future generations and towards humanity as a whole. ... In nature, the believer recognizes the wonderful result of God's creative activity, which we may use responsibly to satisfy our legitimate needs, material or otherwise, while respecting the intrinsic balance of creation. If this vision is lost, we end up either considering nature an untouchable taboo or, on the contrary, abusing it. Neither vision is consonant with the Christian vision of nature as the fruit of God's creation.
>
> *Nature expresses a design of love and truth.* It is prior to us, and it has been given to us by God as the setting for our life. Nature speaks to us of the Creator (cf. Rom. 1:20) and his love for humanity. It is destined to be "recapitulated" in Christ at the end of time (cf. Eph 1:9–10; Col 1:19–20). ... Nature is at our disposal not as "a heap of scattered refuse" [Heraclitus of Ephesus], but as a gift of the Creator who has given it an inbuilt order, enabling man [sic] to draw from it the principles needed in order "to till and keep it" [Gen 2:15]. ... [T]he natural environment is more than raw material to be manipulated at our pleasure; it is a wondrous work of the Creator containing a "grammar" which sets forth ends and criteria for its wise use. (no. 48, emphasis in original)

In relation to agroecology, an especially salient aspect of this passage is how Benedict's account of natural law implicates the entirety of creation and its goodness, wisdom, intelligibility, and integrity. Benedict invokes the balance and order of creation, as well as the presence of principles – even a grammar – that can guide our use of it. (We will return to the language of balance and order below.) As he puts it elsewhere, Benedict believes that there is an "ethical message contained in being, a message that the tradition calls *lex naturalis*, natural moral law."[146] The wisdom pervading creation can orient human life because it reflects the Wisdom in whom all things hold together.[147]

The message Benedict discerns in the creaturely world is therefore not just moral but also theological, speaking to us of its Creator. Benedict weds his account of natural law to foundational theological convictions such as the belief that God is not one being among others but the very ground of all being, the one who brings all creatures into existence and holds them in it by love. To borrow an image from Herbert McCabe, God is like a singer sustaining a song against the silence. But as McCabe himself observes, even this image ultimately falls short. Silence presupposes being, whereas God is the source of being, the one whose action enables all action.[148] Because all creatures are brought into existence and sustained in it by the Creator, they are united by bonds of creaturehood, participating in God's providential wisdom by being the creatures they are created to be. The first message that creation and its creatures speak is therefore that they are not the authors of their own existence. In the words of Hugh of St. Victor, "the whole sensible world is like a kind of book written by the finger of God" and pointing to its Creator (see *Caritas in veritate*, no. 51).[149]

For Benedict, then, creation is a gift of the God who is love and who has been revealed and made flesh in Jesus Christ. It is out of love that God creates all things, sustains them in being, and provides for them. That God gives the gift of creation in common – "to everyone," "to humanity as a whole" – testifies to the love that creates, sustains, provides for, and recapitulates all things. As we saw Gratian state at the outset of this Element, "by natural law, all things are common."

Benedict's account of natural law also signals the unique role and responsibility of humans in creation. Like other creatures, we are part of God's gift of creation and participate in God's providence, but we do so distinctively. For instance, we can learn to conform our provisioning to God's, helping to realize the commonality of the gift by sharing what is in excess of our needs with others. In freedom, we can discern and heed an ecological grammar to guide our tilling and keeping, ensuring the earth's ongoing fruitfulness for future generations.

---

[146] Benedict XVI, "Address to the Participants in the International Congress on Natural Moral Law."
[147] Benedict is not the first to integrate ecological concern into the Catholic social teaching tradition. However, prior to him, we do not find the claim that, if we look with care, the creaturely world has wisdom to teach us about how to live well on this earth. See Groppe, "The Way of Wisdom."
[148] McCabe, "The Myth of God Incarnate," 355.
[149] Hugh of Saint-Victor, *De tribus diebus*, 4.

However, under the conditions of sin, we refuse that conformity and disregard the grammar that sets forth ends and criteria for wise use. This is why Benedict insists on our responsibility toward those whose use and enjoyment of creation is imperiled because of sin: the impoverished who suffer from sin through the deprivation of basic material needs. In the Christian tradition, they are paradigmatically the hungry, the thirsty, the naked, the shelterless, the sick, and the imprisoned (Mt 25:31–46). Moreover, looking beyond the present time, future generations are also at risk because of the damage we have done and continue to do to what God gives in common, which is why Benedict mentions them as well. On Benedict's view, an essential question for any natural law ethic is therefore, how do we use the world in a way that enables us to provide for ourselves and others – especially for those who are excluded from accessing the gifts of creation – both in the present and in the future, ensuring that everyone can make use of what God gives in common?

We have been examining how Benedict situates Catholic social teaching's natural law ethic within a more comprehensive theological framework that centers on God's gift of creation and its message of love as revealed and enfleshed in Jesus Christ. The main argument of *Caritas in veritate* is that love for this truth is the indispensable principle for our wise use of creation. Notice also that Benedict's natural law ethic locates human life within the three fundamental relationships mentioned earlier: with God, with one another, and with the wider creaturely world. Until recently, social teaching's natural law ethic primarily focused on the first two relationships, often neglecting the wider created order.[150] Throughout its development, social teaching has reflected dominant currents in Christian theology and ethics that presuppose and oftentimes explicitly affirm dualisms between humans and the rest of creation, spirit and matter, and culture and nature, associating the former with rationality and the latter with irrationality.[151] As Jean Porter observes, this modern view of the natural law characteristically drives a "wedge" between "rational" humans and "irrational" creation, disregarding or denying not only the continuities between humans and other creatures but also the wider created order as an intelligible expression of divine rationality (Jn 1:1–3).[152] On such a view, creation bears no message and offers no wisdom to guide human life.

---

[150] Pope, "Natural Law in Catholic Social Teaching."

[151] Dupré, *Passage to Modernity*; ITC, *In Search of a Universal Ethic*, sec. 3.3.69–75; French, "With Radical Amazement," 54–67. Carolyn Merchant notes that these dualisms have also been historically tied to divisions between maleness and "lower" forms of human life associated with animality and nature, as well as between civilization and barbarism. Merchant, *The Death of Nature*, 143–144.

[152] The naturalistic fallacy associated with David Hume and G.E. Moore, which holds that moral conclusions cannot be derived from factual premises about nature, presupposes this wedge. See Porter, *Natural and Divine Law*, 26–28, 63, 93.

In contrast, the ecologized natural law ethic Benedict articulates in *Caritas in veritate* integrates the human creature's relation to the rest of creation, in addition to its relation to God and other humans. As we saw earlier, the language social teaching uses for the whole formed by these three fundamental and interwoven relationships is integral ecology, an ecology described by the International Theological Commission as a "deeper understanding of the natural law." It is deeper both because it illuminates the fullness of human relationality and also because it seeks to reach the deepest, most intractable roots of the damage we have done to one another and to the earth.[153]

At the same time, Benedict suggests that this natural law ethic has practical – even agricultural – implications that follow from the commonality of the gift of creation. Acknowledging that God's giving unfolds temporally raises questions about how we care for lands, buildings, and created goods so that they will be available to those who will come after us and who will also need to make use of them. Industrial agriculture operates within a productionist paradigm, often presuming a tradeoff between maintaining agricultural production in the present "to feed a hungry world," on the one hand, and conservation efforts, on the other. In a similar fashion, its advocates often presume a tradeoff between the present and the future, effectively prioritizing the former at the expense of the latter. The inner logic of Benedict's view contrasts with these presumptions, raising questions like, how do we provide for ourselves and for one another in the present, agriculturally and otherwise, so that future generations will not find the earth's soils degraded, its waters depleted, and its habitats for other creatures eliminated? His response is that if we attend carefully to the message of creation, we can learn how to till and keep it well.

The Exemplarity of Ecosystems

How do we provide for ourselves and for one another while working with the grammar of creation? What are the ends and criteria for its wise use? Can the agricultural implications of this ecologized natural law ethic be further specified? Elsewhere, Benedict advocates for laws and policies that affirm smallholder farming families, as well as for agricultural traditions adapted to local ecology and responsive to the cycles and rhythms of nature, but without providing further detail.[154]

---

[153] Francis, *Querida amazonia*, no. 41; Francis, *Laudato si'*, no. 68; ITC, *In Search of a Universal Ethic*, sec. 3.4.82.
[154] Whelan, "The Grammar of Creation."

Within Catholic social teaching, those details emerge more clearly in the writings of Pope Francis. Even before the release of *Laudato si'* in 2015, Francis reiterates Benedict's call for greater attention to the "'grammar' inscribed in nature" and its relevance to agriculture. For instance, in his first World Day of Peace message in 2014, Francis acknowledges that the most fundamental feature of that grammar is that creation is a gift given to the human family in common, and that God means for the gift to benefit all people. Attending to creation's grammar can help us use and preserve the gift so all people can enjoy it, while also prompting greater recognition of "the beauty, finality, and usefulness of every living being and its place in the ecosystem." In the message, Francis also singles out agriculture as "the primary productive sector with the crucial vocation of cultivating and protecting natural resources in order to feed humanity."[155]

While Francis clearly privileges human creatures, he also acknowledges the existence of other creatures, their integration into ecosystems, and their purposes apart from human use. As Carmody Grey has argued, throughout his writings, Francis refuses "the negative contrast between human and nonhuman," regarding it as "a false contrast." She observes that, according to Francis, "We either value both, or we value neither."[156]

In *Laudato si'*, Francis develops these points in relationship to what he calls the "technocratic paradigm" and its "throwaway culture" (nos. 16, 20–22, 101–36), drawing a contrast between them and the wisdom of ecosystems and the need to cultivate an alternative regenerative culture. As noted earlier, a hallmark of the technocratic paradigm is a technique of mastery whereby the human subject, through scientific and experimental procedures, exerts possession and control over objects, as if they are formless and completely manipulatable. For those beholden to this paradigm, the wider creaturely world is like a blank page, bearing no message, with no ecological grammar to discern or imitate. Given the kinds of creatures we are and the freedom we have over our actions, it is certainly possible for us to refuse such discernment and imitation. But the consequence, as Francis sees it, is damage. Because the world is primarily a reservoir of manipulable and extractable raw material for the technocratic paradigm, the associated culture devotes little thought or practical attention to the reabsorption or reuse of its by-products. Unsurprisingly, this culture therefore tends to waste what it uses, which is why Francis calls it a "throwaway culture." As we would therefore expect, it is a culture whose agriculture tills without keeping (nos. 21, 23, 34, 41).[157]

---

[155] Francis, "Fraternity, the Foundation and Pathway to Peace," no. 9.
[156] Grey, "The Only Creature God Willed for Its Own Sake," 874.
[157] Whelan, "The Peril and the Promise of Agriculture."

Christianity and Agroecology 41

Throughout *Laudato si'*, Francis argues for an approach to agriculture – and to the practical arts more generally – in terms resonant with agroecology. Rather than regard the creaturely world as a blank page or a reservoir of extractable raw material, Francis, like Benedict, draws on an ancient strand of theological reflection we have already encountered, one that regards the creaturely world as a book whose pages are filled with the words of creatures that manifest the divine wisdom (nos. 12, 85, 239).[158] In true agroecological fashion, Francis directs us to the exemplarity of ecosystems and their wisdom, envisioning agricultural and other human arts imitative of ecology. "Plants synthesize nutrients which feed herbivores," he observes. "These in turn become food for carnivores, which produce significant quantities of organic waste which give rise to new generations of plants." Indeed, the very notion of "waste" – in the sense of useless by-products – is closely linked to industrialism and is inapplicable to ecosystems. In ecosystems, sunlight, water, and minerals, not fossil fuels, supply the energy, and what creatures discard is never wasted but recycled and reused by other creatures.[159] Francis contends that by modeling production on the circularity of ecosystems, we can till while keeping, reducing the use of non-renewable sources, moderating consumption, and enhancing efficiency. The vision of the encyclical therefore closely coheres with agroecology's approach of working with ecological principles and processes. Francis holds out hope for a form of economy that prioritizes life and, by so doing, protects, sustains, and regenerates its sources and all that enables it (no. 190). "A serious consideration" of how we can better learn to imitate the circularity of ecosystems, Francis contends, "would be one way of counteracting the throwaway culture which affects the entire planet" (no. 22).

In the remainder of *Laudato si'*, Francis reinforces these agroecological resonances while articulating additional iconvergences. He celebrates the extravagance, proliferation, and diversity of creaturely life, which testifies to the God who is love and who creates in love.[160] Francis laments the role of humans in creation's damage and destruction – a hallmark of humankind's refusal to keep the earth, as well as till it (nos. 8, 12, 24, 32–42, 84, 87, 134). He urges "greater investment ... in research aimed at understanding more fully the functioning of ecosystems" (no. 42) – the kind of research agroecologists conduct. Like agroecology, Francis champions "a sustainable and diversified agriculture" based on complex crop rotations (nos. 164, 180), epitomized by

---

[158] Peter Harrison provides a history of this tradition in *The Bible, Protestantism, and the Rise of Natural Science*.

[159] Although Francis does not mention it, it is significant that within ecosystems, even the death of creatures becomes a source of life for others.

[160] Jenkins, "Biodiversity and Salvation."

communities of smallholder producers who preserve local ecosystems. Echoing a point often made by agroecologists, Francis observes that many of these smallholders practice an agriculture that, despite its marginality, still "feeds the greater part of the world's peoples, using a modest amount of land and producing less waste, be it in small agricultural parcels, in orchards and gardens, hunting and wild harvesting or local fishing" (nos. 129, 180). Moreover, like agroecology, Francis recognizes that agriculture has a politics. It is impossible to practice a biodiverse agriculture that preserves local ecosystems and nourishes people if communities do not have land or if their access to it is threatened (nos. 93–95, 130–136).[161] Given both lack of access to land and current threats to it, Francis calls for "a new and universal solidarity" between peoples and across generations – a solidarity, he adds, that we are made for, because we were made by and for love (nos. 14, 58, 158–162, 172). An entailment of such solidarity – often insisted on by agroecologists – is that when studying diversified agroecosystems, we cannot neglect local cultures and traditions. Much like the dialogue of wisdoms that agroecology proposes, Francis favors exchanges that respectfully listen to and integrate both "scientific-technical language and the language of the people" (nos. 143–146).[162] Across all these aspects of *Laudato si'*, then, resonances and convergences with agroecology abound.

While the developments we have been tracing within Catholic social teaching certainly point in practical directions and converge with agroecology, social teaching has not explicitly mentioned or endorsed agroecology. Generally speaking, the tradition tends to be reticent regarding particular plans of implementation or specific socio-ecological parameters because social teaching is a genre of moral theological thought that self-consciously limits itself, as Paul VI explains in his apostolic letter *Octogesima adveniens* (1971), to general "principles of reflection, norms of judgement, and directives for action" (no. 4). To paraphrase the Salvadoran martyr and saint, Óscar Romero, the language of the church does not "invade" other fields and has no technical revolution to offer.[163] Its primary gift to the world is the Gospel. Nevertheless, social teaching recognizes that it needs other disciplines, drawing on their wisdom to interpret the world in the light of the Gospel and to guide the action of Christians and all people of good will.[164] Hence, while social teaching's natural law ethic clearly has important implications for agriculture, it is in keeping with the genre of social teaching not to specify those implications, leaving it to its adherents "to

---

[161] Francis develops this theme in his addresses to the World Meetings of Popular Movements.

[162] Pope Francis, *Let Us Dream*, 128–129.

[163] Romero, *Homilías*, vol. 4, 501. The phrase "technical revolution" is from John Paul II, *Sollicitudo rei socialis*, no. 41.

[164] John Paul II, *Centesimus annus*, no. 54.

discern the options and commitments which are called for in order to bring about the social, political, and economic changes seen in many cases to be urgently needed," in the words of Paul VI (no. 4).

Although Catholic social teaching does not explicitly mention or endorse agroecology, many Catholic communities and people of faith throughout the world have. While often unappreciated, Catholics have long participated in the development of agroecology as a field, especially in Latin America,[165] as well as in the popular social movements like those that gathered in Nyéléni.[166] Today, both within the Catholic Church and outside of it, initiatives are proliferating in response to the call of *Laudato si'* to care for our common home, further evidence of the moral commonalities between social teaching and agroecology.[167]

Divergences

We have been exploring the convergences between Catholic social teaching and agroecology, principally in relation to their shared discernment of ecological principles and processes that enable us to care for the creaturely world while providing for ourselves and others in the process. As we have seen, Benedict contends that creation has a grammar that offers ends and criteria for wise use, and Francis develops this idea further by suggesting that agriculture – and economic life more generally – should pattern itself on the circularity of ecosystems. Doing so can help resist a technocratic paradigm and its throwaway culture.

Amid these convergences, we have also noted divergences. Especially crucial in this regard is the theological character of social teaching's natural law ethic. This ethic conceives of human life as participating in a comprehensive ecology that joins our relationships to God, one another, and the rest of creation into a whole that it refers to as integral ecology. By contrast, agroecology as a discipline is not explicitly theological, tending to focus on our relationships to the world and to one another – although some agroecologists have now begun

---

[165] Hernández Castillo, "Organic Growers"; Botelho, Cardoso, and Otsuki, "I Made a Pact with God, with Nature, and with Myself'"; Mier y Terán Giménez Cacho et al., "Bringing Agroecology to Scale"; Calderón et al., "Agroecology-Based Farming Provides Grounds for More Resilient Livelihoods among Smallholders in Western Guatemala"; Travieso, "Reason to Hope."

[166] Pope Francis, "Address to the Participants in the World Meeting of Popular Movements"; Pope Francis, "Address to the Participants in the Second World Meeting of Popular Movements"; Pope Francis, "Address to the Participants in the Third World Meeting of Popular Movements."

[167] See "*Laudato si'* Movement"; Whelan, *Theological Foundations for Agriculture According to Laudato si'*.

to argue that agroecology should not exclude theological conviction on principle.[168]

We have also already examined another significant divergence: Catholic social teaching's embrace of an idealized ecology. In *Caritas in veritate*, Benedict mentions the intrinsic balance of creation and its inbuilt order (no. 48). Similarly, throughout *Laudato si'*, Francis repeatedly alludes not only to natural balances but also to ecological equilibria and harmonies (nos. 10, 34–35, 57, 66, 68, 210, 225). Admittedly, parsing the precise meaning of such language is not always easy because, on both Benedict's and Francis's terms, these are balances, equilibria, and harmonies that explicitly include human beings and their relation to God, as well as depend on theological distinctions between creation as originally created, fallen, and redeemed. However, despite these caveats, social teaching's ecologized natural law ethic clearly remains beholden to an idealized ecology.[169] The tradition registers little recognition that ecosystems are time-bound, that they undergo constant change, and that, even apart from the presence of human creatures, they are characterized by both stabilities and instabilities, symbioses and conflicts, harmonies and dissonances.

Additionally, while Catholic social teaching certainly notes the existence of death and suffering in the wider creaturely world, the tradition tends to associate these phenomena exclusively with human interference or exploitation. In other words, social teaching does not regard death and suffering as constitutive to the balance, equilibrium, or order to which it appeals. Francis is representative of this tendency when he begins *Laudato si'* by telling us that "our Sister, Mother Earth, who sustains and governs us … cries out to us because of the harm we have inflicted on her by our irresponsible use and abuse of the goods with which God has endowed her" (nos. 1–2). There is no disputing that humans have inflicted such harm, and that we are now, for instance, the major driver of habitat destruction, species extinction, climate change, and numerous other forms of ecological damage. But neither in this passage nor elsewhere does Francis or social teaching more generally note the creaturely cries and groans that are always and everywhere present within ecosystems apart from human use and abuse (Rom 8:22). Nor do they note how the creaturely world is, in Alfred Lord Tennyson's famous phrase from *In Memoriam*, red in tooth and claw (sec. 56, l. 15).[170]

---

[168] Victor Toledo thinks agroecological thought should acknowledge the spiritualities of agroecological practitioners, which often speak of the earth as our mother and of human life as dependent on, governed by, and duty-bound towards her. Toledo, "Agroecology and Spirituality." See also Whelan, "Agroecology's Moral Vision"; Giraldo, *Ecología política de la agricultura*.

[169] Deane-Drummond, "Joining in the Dance," 211; Deane-Drummond, "*Laudato si'* and the Natural Sciences"; Hibbs, *A Theology of Creation*.

[170] Tennyson, *In Memoriam*.

While the groaning of creation is perhaps most perceptible in the existence of predators like wolves, leopards, and lions, whose teeth and claws are soaked with the blood of their prey, agroecology draws our attention to quieter, more hidden forms of death that constitute and sustain creaturely life. However, we need not be agroecologists to perceive this truth about the world. Anyone who considers the soil of a well-functioning agroecosystem will notice that it is a graveyard, a site of countless creaturely deaths, as well as lives and ecological processes that arise from them. Death is constitutive of the soil's fertility and its ability to support diverse, creaturely life, a reality that is inextricable from the balance, order, equilibria, and harmony described by social teaching.

It is not just that there is death in the creaturely world but that there is no creaturely world, at least as we know it, without it. Death is an essential condition for the lives of other creatures – the bacteria and fungi that break down the bodies of dead organisms, the plants that take up the dissolved organic matter and nutrients, the pastured animals that eat the grass sustained by the fertility of the soil, and the humans that eat these and other creatures. As mentioned earlier, agroecology relies on biological control rather than pesticides to control insect herbivores, mimicking predator–prey dynamics in natural ecosystems by encouraging the presence of natural enemies, such as predators, parasites, and pathogens that feed on the insects that eat crops. The higher balance agroecologists foster in agroecosystems depends on these and numerous other similar dynamics. Simply put, there is no escaping the reality that creaturely life in this world depends on death. Our choice, then, is not *whether* or not to depend on death but *how* we choose to do so. Agroecologists receive death by acknowledging it, working with it and processes dependent on it in order to foster ecological goods. By so doing, agroecologists are, effectively, managing death for the good of the whole farm, as well as for those of us who live from its fruits.

At least until this point in its development, Catholic social teaching has remained silent on the inherent and constitutive inseparability of creaturely death to the grammar of the natural environment and the exemplarity of natural ecosystems. Given Pope Francis's heavy reliance on St. Francis's *Canticle of the Creatures* in *Laudato si'*, the lack of substantive, theological discussion of "Sister, Bodily Death" for creatures other than humans is noteworthy.[171] As a result, social teaching's ecologized natural law still remains, as I suggested earlier, insufficiently ecologized.

The Catholic social teaching tradition is not alone in its embrace of an idealized ecology. Lisa Sideris has influentially critiqued the extent to which much

---

[171] Francis of Assisi, "Canticle of the Creatures," 114.

contemporary ecological theology and ethics similarly subscribes to a view of creation as pervaded by harmony, interconnection, and interdependence – what she calls "the ecological model." Various, distinct currents within contemporary theology and ethics employ the ecological model, and all of them characteristically evade realities like disharmony, conflict, suffering, and death.[172] Although she does not make the connection herself, Sideris's depiction of the ecological model is quite similar to social teaching's ecologized natural law. According to Sideris, those employing the ecological model often find a moral and theological message of harmony, interconnection, and interdependence within creation, which they regard as having normative import for our relationships with human and other creatures. While there are certainly important differences between the ecological model Sideris critiques and social teaching's ecologized natural law, both share a simplified and idealized version of ecology that fails to attend to important truths about the creaturely world.

Given the complexities and ambiguities that engagement with the ecological sciences unearths for theologians and ethicists, a growing number of voices advocate abandonment of natural law altogether and any conception of natural normativity along with it. In a volume entitled *Religion and the New Ecology: Environmental Responsibility in a World in Flux*, editors David Lodge and Christopher Hamlin take aim at appeals to ecology and natural normativity by theologians and ethicists. Notions like ecological stability, balance, and equilibrium, they argue, are no longer adequate in the face of an ecology of flux. Without these notions to serve as guides, what is left to orient us in our use of the world? "This new ecology [of flux] is terrifying," they write, "because it exposes the inadequacy of our normative systems," forcing us to relinquish the mistaken belief that the natural world has any wisdom to impart.[173] In another volume, *Without Nature? A New Condition for Theology*, David Albertson asks whether the loss of nature as "an ecological and biological constant" plunges Christian theology into a new and seemingly unprecedented predicament, making any natural law ethic untenable. Albertson is thinking here not just about what the ecology of flux, with its disruption of previously held stabilities, teaches us about the world, but also about the technological power humankind now wields over terrestrial life. In the judgment of these scholars, taking the ecological sciences seriously yields a vision of the creaturely world that conveys no message and offers no guidance for how we should live, undermining any account of natural law.[174]

---

[172] Sideris, *Environmental Ethics, Ecological Theology, and Natural Selection*.
[173] Lodge, *Religion and the New Ecology*, 7–9.
[174] There are also important currents in modern theology – Catholic and Protestant alike – that explicitly critique natural law as a legitimate source for moral reflection or convey little interest in creation other than humankind. See Porter, *Natural and Divine Law*, 15–16, 30–32, 64–65.

The foregoing therefore presents us with a dilemma. If the problem with Catholic social teaching's ecologized natural law ethic is its insufficient ecologization, the problem with these critics' understanding of ecology is that it leaves little room for natural law or the conviction that the world bears a message. Is there a constructive path forward? In the remainder of this section, I suggest that there is, and that a more substantive engagement by Catholic social teaching with agroecology can address both these problems, and in so doing, contribute to the further revision and development of social teaching itself.

Toward a Deeper Understanding of the Natural Law

Catholic social teaching's natural law ethic seeks to remedy the damage we have done to our common home, radically expanding the category of ecology to include our relationships to God, one another, and the wider creation. However, while such an integral ecology is irreducible to science, it should nevertheless be accountable to it. Agroecology not only helps social teaching maintain this accountability but also conveys wisdom about the creaturely world and how to live well within it, which social teaching can draw on. But what kind of wisdom does agroecology offer?

First and foremost, it offers practical wisdom. A central contention of this Element has been that agroecology gives Christians and people of good will practical tools for tilling and keeping the earth. For instance, the central priority of agroecological management is fostering more complex and diverse agroecosystems due to the manifold ecological goods that derive from doing so. For those interested in cultivating these agroecosystems themselves or in learning to recognize and support those people and communities who do, agroecology offers important guidance. In these and other ways, agroecology aids us in living more deeply into our vocation to provide for ourselves and one another while also caring for God's creation.

Besides practical wisdom, this Element has also shown that agroecology imparts a kind of theoretical wisdom. I have argued that agroecology can assist Catholic social teaching in better conceptualizing and articulating its ecologized natural law ethic, loosening the hold idealized ecology still has on this and other moral theological traditions. We have seen that, rather than preserving or restoring stable equilibria, natural balances, or pristine harmonies, agroecology's ecological grammar prioritizes ecological principles and processes that can be implemented in different ways. The resulting agroecosystems are more adaptable in the face of dynamic, unpredictable, and uncontrollable climatic conditions than industrial ones. Crucially, adaptation of agroecologically managed agroecosystems to those conditions sometimes involves the persistence of underlying relationships, while at other times, their transformation. The upshot is that whatever equilibrium, balance, or harmony characterizes agroecologically managed agroecosystems at any given time and place, there are multiple possible states and paths to them. Moreover, we have also seen how agroecology involves working with creaturely death as a constitutive and productive feature of agroecosystems. Instead of ignoring or denying this reality, agroecologists face it directly, acknowledging its centrality to our provisioning, working to manage death and the ecological goods resulting from death.

Accordingly, if Catholic social teaching remains committed to the language of equilibria, balance, and harmony in its characterization of the creaturely world, agroecology can help us grasp why that language requires more careful qualification and nuance. However, this does not imply that social teaching must abandon its appeal to the grammar of creation. Instead, social teaching can learn from agroecology's own discernment of a kindred ecological grammar in the midst of ecological dynamism, instability, and creaturely suffering and death, allowing the approach of agroecology and related fields to inform and shape social teaching's own approach. In a similar vein, while Francis rightly observes that our Sister, Mother Earth, is crying out to us because of the damage we have done through using and abusing her gifts, social teaching must more readily acknowledge that this use and abuse deepens the cries of a creation already groaning (Rom 8:22).[175]

Against those who argue that ecological science exposes the inadequacy of any normativity derived from the creaturely world, agroecology therefore serves as an ally to Catholic social teaching by suggesting an alternative way forward. While agroecology integrates ecological and agronomic science, the discipline does not operate as if doing so silences the world's message or undermines care for our common home. However, a key implication of agroecology's discernment of an ecological grammar written in the world, like a message we can learn to read, is that the message does not simply interpret itself. Learning to read it well presumes formation within a community of able interpreters, as well as the gradual accumulation of practical knowledge gathered by those communities across time. Nor is the natural normativity that agroecology discerns the discipline's only moral norm. Practitioners and communities engaged in agroecological work often give voice to numerous additional convictions, among them: that the world and its creatures and processes are not merely commodities to be bought and

---

[175] Johnson, *Ask the Beasts*, 189–190.

sold or raw material to be extracted and manipulated, but rather a source of life and goodness worth protecting and defending; that the world comprises an intelligible whole within which there is wisdom to discover that can guide our agriculture; and finally, that the world is not the work of human hands, and that we, like other creatures, depend on it for our survival and flourishing, and should therefore keep it in our tilling of it. Agroecology's ecological grammar often comes to us intertwined with these and other convictions.[176]

All this demonstrates that, in response to critics of its reliance on an idealized ecology, Catholic social teaching has available sources of wisdom to draw on, and the tradition can learn from disciplines like agroecology regarding a more adequate ecologization of its natural law ethic. However, if social teaching embarks on such an undertaking, it will not need to start from scratch, because the tradition already shares significant moral commonalities with agroecology related to the natural law. We have traced how, in recent decades, social teaching has arrived at the conviction that the wider created world has a grammar that can guide us in its wise use, and that there is an exemplarity to natural ecosystems from which we can learn. What agroecology therefore represents is a dialogue of wisdom among scientists, farmers, and movement activists who similarly appeal to an ecological grammar and who have long been engaged in the work of tilling and keeping to which social teaching now calls its adherents. Agroecology offers Catholic social teaching a compelling example of how to uphold such a grammar without idealizing it.

In this way, agroecology is a gift that Catholic social teaching can receive with gratitude, extending an opportunity for further practical realization of the tradition's own commitment to integral ecology, along with the conceptual clarification and deepening of that holistic ecology. If this opportunity is accepted, what will result is admittedly a humbler account of the natural law, in which the creaturely world does not speak in the language of easily discernable equilibria, balances, and harmonies. Rather, as we have seen in these pages, the message of the creaturely world is complex and multifaceted, requiring interpreters who can integrate it into a larger, more comprehensive vision. Ultimately, what results will be a natural law ethic that has the immeasurable benefit of being truer to the kinds of creatures we are and the world we inhabit, one that can help us provide for ourselves and for one another while also sharing what God gives in common.

---

[176] Whelan, "Agroecology's Moral Vision."

4 Science-Engaged Theology and Theologically-Engaged Science

Introduction

This Element has introduced Christians and people of good will to agroecology. Previous sections have shown how agroecology advances the vocation to till and keep the earth. Additionally, we have explored how Catholic social teaching can constructively engage with and even learn from agroecology, contributing to the tradition's development and perhaps even serving as an example for other moral theological traditions to follow.

This concluding section steps back to reflect on the enquiry pursued in these pages as a form of science-engaged theology, as well as some of the complexities encountered when drawing on the sciences as a source for moral theological reflection. We will also revisit the issue raised in the previous section regarding Catholic social teaching's embrace of idealized ecology and the need for social teaching, like other forms of moral theological reflection, to address death directly. My contention is that addressing death is imperative, not simply for the sake of scientific accountability, but also because of the properly moral theological questions that death raises. While these pages have primarily focused on agroecology's contribution to Catholic social teaching, we will conclude by considering social teaching's unique contribution to agroecology's dialogue of wisdoms and what agroecology might learn from engagement with traditions like it.

Science-Engaged Theology

As indicated at the outset, by relying on agroecology as a source of insight for Catholic social teaching, our enquiry bears obvious relation to what is known today as science-engaged theology, a subfield within the broader field of theology and science. John Perry and Joanna Leidenhag explain that "science-engaged theology aims to serve as a reminder to theologians that the local tools and products of the sciences ought to be sources for theological reasoning.... The basic principle of science-engaged theology is that whenever theologians make claims about created, empirical realities, they should incorporate the insights of empirical investigation into their analysis."[177]

The authors describe this approach as a kind of *memento naturam* (Latin for "remember nature"), explicitly alluding to the ancient tradition of *memento mori* ("remember death") that took widespread artistic form throughout

---

[177] Perry and Leidenhag, *Science-Engaged Theology*, 1. See also Perry and Leidenhag, "What Is Science-Engaged Theology?"

medieval and early modern Europe in images of skulls and other depictions of mortality. Just as people have long reminded one another in word and image to remember that they are dust and to dust they will return (Gen 3:19), Perry and Leidenhag contend that theologians and ethicists also need reminders that their work sometimes involves empirical claims about the world. When that happens, theologians and ethicists do well to remember nature, turning to scientific tools and methods for assistance. In this way, science can serve as a valuable source of understanding for theology, just as I have argued that agroecology does for Catholic social teaching.[178]

At the same time, we have also observed that the agricultural sciences do not speak in a single, clear voice, nor do they only address empirical realities. While it is true that theological and ethical claims often come entangled with empirical ones, it is also true that empirical claims often come entangled with cosmological, anthropological, and ethical ones. We have seen how the agricultural sciences present conflicting visions about the world, the human, and the way we should live – assumptions that must be recognized and critically interrogated both before and during any engagement with the sciences. To paraphrase Carmody Grey, the empirical is not a discretely identifiable and bounded domain but is diversely construed, and this diverse construal demands our attention as we receive scientific findings.[179] Consequently, Perry and Leidenhag's exposition of science-engaged theology raises numerous issues regarding how moral theological traditions like Catholic social teaching discern which of the sciences to engage, as well as how to engage them.

Agroecologists, in particular, are acutely well aware of the conflicting visions within the agricultural sciences. As noted in Section 1, Vandermeer attributes this to fundamental differences in philosophy, formation, and characteristic questions. Although not discussed in that section, Vandermeer's main example of these differences is the Guatemalan entomologist Helda Morales's work among the Cakchiquel, a Mayan indigenous people of the Guatemalan highlands who continue to practice *milpa* agriculture to this day.[180] This example further underscores the diverse construal of the empirical and its implications for science-engaged theology.

At the outset of her research, Morales conducted a survey in which she asked farmers, *do you have pests in your* milpa?, to which the majority responded that they did not. However, after conducting field observations and cataloguing many insect herbivores in the fields, widely considered "pests" of corn, she

---

[178] Perry and Leidenhag, *Science-Engaged Theology*, 1–2.
[179] Grey, "A Theologian's Perspective on Science-Engaged Theology," 492, 494.
[180] Morales and Perfecto, "Traditional Knowledge and Pest Management in the Guatemalan Highlands"; Morales, "Pest Management in Traditional Tropical Ecosystems."

added a new question to the survey: *are there insects that eat the* milpa? In response, all the farmers answered affirmatively and identified them. Subsequently, instead of focusing on how Cakchiquel farmers dealt with "pest" problems, as she learned from her traditional agronomic training, her research shifted to understanding why they did not experience significant problems in the first place and why damage to crops by insect herbivores did not compromise the harvest. This shift highlights differences in agroecosystem design and management but also deeper differences related to, in Morales's words, "our concept of pest."[181] According to these Cakchiquel farmers, not all insect herbivores, even when present in their fields, are considered "pests." Within the agricultural sciences, this simple designation is entangled with conflicting accounts of the empirical, such as the nature of these creatures, our relation to them, and the technologies we use to manage them. Additionally, it is also entangled with power relationships, especially in places like the Guatemalan highlands, where agricultural science can often be a powerful and monological presence, with agronomists standing as the voice of reason over and against what they regard as irrationality, backwardness, and traditionalism.

By highlighting the diverse construal of the empirical within the agricultural sciences, Morales's work returns us to a recurrent theme in this Element: discernment. We have explored this theme in relation to agroecology's discovery of an ecological grammar. However, the distinct cultures within the agricultural sciences emphasize the need for a form of discernment that raises and reflects on questions like, why engage agroecology rather than industrial agricultural science? How do we adjudicate conflicts regarding empirical reality within scientific fields? More broadly, how do we determine which sciences are amenable sources for theological and moral reasoning, especially when certain sciences, as seen in the case of industrial agricultural science, may obscure rather than illuminate our understanding of the world and how to live well within it?

Given the Christian vocation to care for God's creation, these concerns are not peripheral. In his seminal essay, "The Historical Roots of Our Ecologic Crisis," historian Lynn White Jr. influentially argued that the ecological crisis partially results from the fusion of modern scientific knowledge and technology, which has endowed humankind with unprecedented power to control and manipulate the world and its creatures.[182] While scholars have rightly contested White's argument and its legacy, at least on this point,[183] White's argument

---

[181] Morales and Perfecto, "Traditional Knowledge and Pest Management in the Guatemalan Highlands," 53.
[182] White, "The Historical Roots of Our Ecologic Crisis."
[183] See Jenkins, *Ecologies of Grace*, 10–15; "After Lynn White."

resonates with *Laudato si'*. There, Francis characterizes the science associated with technocratic paradigm as itself "a technique of possession, mastery and transformation" (no. 106), viewing the world and its creatures as formless and completely manipulatable. From this perspective, science is not just a tool, whose methods and insights can be drawn on as a source of understanding. It can also sometimes generate a warped and reductive knowledge that does not assist us in the tasks of *memento naturam* or the cultivation of care. The assumptions of such science should be critiqued, a stance that agroecology takes toward industrial agricultural science.

What all this suggests is the need for discernment prior to any theological engagement with specific sciences.[184] In this Element, Catholic social teaching's natural law ethic itself has played a crucial role in this regard, helping to identify agroecology as an interlocutor and to recognize resonances with social teaching's own understanding of the empirical. That natural law ethic has also served to surface and critique some of industrial agriculture's underlying assumptions. For this reason, while theologians and ethicists should *memento naturam*, we must also remember that the message of creaturely reality is not so clear and unambiguous that it can be easily read off the surface of things. Even within the sciences, the empirical is often entwined with many other assumptions and commitments. In these pages, social teaching's natural law ethic has aided in critically examining assumptions and commitments operative within the agricultural sciences. Consequently, while the language of the church must not invade other fields, it also cannot simply defer to their deliverances. Given the church's language, there are prior and essential discernments to be made, which has guided my approach in these pages.

The Gift of Death

The foregoing notwithstanding, theological engagement with the sciences can lead to critical appropriation of select perspectives and insights, as this Element has sought to demonstrate. As I have argued, agroecology can help loosen the grip of an idealized ecology on Catholic social teaching, thereby repairing and renewing the tradition. In this way, agroecology serves as a legitimate source of wisdom for social teaching, instigating both self-critique and a more thorough ecologization – and perhaps even the development of a deeper understanding of the natural law.

To this end, an aspect of Catholic social teaching's natural law ethic that requires much more sustained reflection is the significance of the inherent and

---

[184] Perry and Leidenhag are aware of this, mentioning the need for prudence in engaging the sciences. See Perry and Leidenhag, *Science-Engaged Theology*, 48.

constitutive inseparability of death from the ecological grammar that gives ends and criteria for good use. The task of *memento naturam* points to how, at least in the order of our experience and knowledge of the world, life depends on death, as does the productivity, functioning, and potential exemplarity of ecosystems. This reality might make it seem, in a reversal of the traditional Augustinian formula that evil is parasitic on the good (*privatio boni*), that the good of life is parasitic on the evil of creaturely death.[185]

Catholic social teaching is not alone among moral theological traditions in failing to grapple adequately with this reality and the challenges it poses. Yet, if traditions like social teaching continue to appeal to ecology, they must more explicitly reflect on the death of plants and non-human animals within the wider creaturely world. If life depends on death, does that mean death is not wholly evil? Is it part of the created order? Or is life itself a tarnished good because of its entanglement with death? Death is an empirical reality that raises these and other moral theological questions.

Writing during a time when ecological science was first emerging and highlighting the ubiquity of death in the natural world,[186] Tennyson posed a related question in *In Memoriam*: 'Are God and Nature then at strife?' (sec. 55, l. 5). Nature's redness in tooth and claw "shrieks" against the "creed" that "God is love indeed" and that love is "Creation's final law." For Tennyson, the message contained in the structures of nature is profoundly ambiguous, not reflecting a God of love who creates in love. Instead, "ravine" – preying, plundering, and devouring – appears to be the natural law (sec. 56, ll. 13–16).[187] J.R. Illingworth aptly summarizes the stakes in the influential collection *Lux Mundi* (1888): "The universality of pain throughout the animal world, reaching back into the distant ages of geology, and involved in the very structure of the animal organism, is without doubt among the most serious problems the Theist has to face."[188]

Regardless of where one ranks it, the suffering and death of plants and other animals is a theological problem that has garnered significant attention in recent years. Holmes Rolston III, Christopher Southgate, Bethany Sollereder, and Neil Messer, among others, have grappled with this particular form of the problem of evil, principally in relation to the science of evolutionary biology.[189] Biological evolution by natural selection proliferates life on earth and produces the vast diversity of ecosystems and creatures – realities that underpin agroecology's

---

[185] Augustine, *Confessions*, bk. 7, nos. 3–5.   [186] Parham, *Green Man Hopkins*, 77–79.
[187] Tennyson, *In Memoriam*.   [188] Quoted in Southgate, *The Groaning of Creation*, 1.
[189] See Rolston III, "Naturalizing and Systematizing Evil"; Southgate, *The Groaning of Creation*; Sollereder, *God, Evolution, and Animal Suffering*. Messer offers a survey of this literature in *Science in Theology*, 65–98.

whole approach to tilling and keeping and its cultivation of biodiverse agroecosystems. The pervasiveness of death, as well as its inextricability from life, presses the issue of the Creator's relation to it.

Many difficult questions emerge from this line of reflection. In the crucial passage from *Laudato si'* just cited, Francis suggests that, as a consequence of sin, "the originally harmonious relationship between human beings and nature became conflictual" (no. 66, citing Gen 3:17–19). What relationship does this conflict have with death and its role in fostering creaturely life as we know it? Did the original harmony include the death of plants and animals? Is some or all such death constitutive of creation and its original harmony? If so, how does this cohere with God's declaration that creation is "very good" (Gen. 1:31), since death seems to be a kind of evil and thus implies a lack of goodness? Alternatively, is all or some death a result of the fall, whether human or angelic, and part of creation's groaning from sin? Even if incapable of sin, are such creatures damaged by sin, and if so, how? Does this damage include death? If it does, how should we understand the fall of humans in relation to it? The evolutionary record indicates plant and animal death as part of life on earth from the beginning, long before humans emerged, making it difficult to regard death as a consequence of human sin or conflict arising from it.[190] Accounts of the angelic fall appear to accommodate more easily the existence of plant and non-human animal death.[191] However, an angelic fall introduces additional questions, such as, how should we understand human culpability for sin if human life commences in a cosmos that is already fallen?

Death's relation to God's creation of the heavens and the earth is also tied to the question of death's relation to God's recreation of all things in Christ and the Holy Spirit. What place do creatures like plants and non-human animals that have died have in God's ultimate purpose for the creation? What is their final end? Do they share in the resurrection? In *Laudato si'*, Francis depicts the "harmony ... with all creatures" found in figures like St. Francis as a "healing" of sin's damage to creation, a return to creation's original harmony (no. 66).[192] This passage prompts many additional questions about the nature of these harmonies, their interrelationships, and what harmony, if any, is possible in this interim time between our beginning and final end. What is clear is that, against the majority position in the Christian tradition, which has held that such creatures have no place in heaven,[193] Pope Francis believes that the common home we share with them on earth has a common destiny – "with us and

---

[190] Cavanaugh and Smith, *Evolution and the Fall*.
[191] Griffiths offers a defense of the angelic fall in *Decreation*, 131–135. See also Michael Lloyd's essays, "Are Animals Fallen?" and "The Humanity of Fallenness."
[192] See Vauchez, *Francis of Assisi*, 271–282.   [193] Griffiths, *Decreation*, 265–296.

through us" – in the resurrection. In *Laudato si'*, he describes this ultimate harmony, where God heals and transfigures the damage done to creation (nos. 83, 243, 244), with God's words in Rev 21:5, "I make all things new" (no. 243). It is a harmony in which, as we also read in Revelation, "every tear" will be wiped away, and "death will be no more" (Rev 21:4).

The idea that death will one day be no more suggests that death is an artifact of the fall. But this is difficult to reconcile with the empirical realities that inform a natural law ethic – realities that, as we have seen in our consideration of agroecology, point to the crucial role of death in fostering creaturely life as we know it. An alternative is to consider God the author of death.

To sum up, life's dependence on death, along with the related tangle of issues, suggests that a natural law ethic based primarily or exclusively on empirical realities cannot escape a profoundly ambiguous message. It is unclear if this message even points to a Creator. If it does, it is a Creator who is either the author of death or powerless to create otherwise.

Needless to say, this is not how Catholic social teaching understands its natural law ethic or the God to whom it testifies. Instead, social teaching's presumption is that, in Porter's words, the deliverances of nature alone are insufficient and must therefore be "supplemented, complemented, or reformulated in light of other sources for moral knowledge."[194] Clearly, Francis, like Benedict before him, takes seriously those deliverances, calling the creaturely world "a magnificent book in which God speaks to us and grants us a glimpse of his infinite beauty and goodness" (*Laudato si'*, no. 12, see also *Caritas in veritate* no. 51). However, the tradition holds that nature is not the only book through which God speaks to us. Nor is the book of nature as important as the book of scripture for revealing who God is, God's dealings with the world, or even creation's own witness to God. The two books must be read together, the book of nature in light of the book of scripture.[195] An important rationale for this hermeneutic is that, in the creaturely world we experience, the strong often prey on the weak – like a lioness teaching her cubs to hunt by catching, wounding, and releasing a vulnerable antelope for them to practice. In contrast, the advent of Jesus Christ reveals a different message: of the God who creates in love and sustains all creatures in it (*Laudato si'*, nos. 77, 96). The Creator counts even sparrows – and antelopes – and provides for them (Lk 12:6, Mt 6:26). Jesus brings good news to the poor and oppressed (Lk 4:18), and his life enfleshes the mercy of "just as you did it to one of the least ... you did it to me" (Mt 25:40). For this reason, if we are followers of the one in whom all things hold together

---

[194] Porter, *Nature as Reason*, 136.   [195] Second Vatican Council, *Dei verbum*, nos. 3, 6, 9–10.

(Col 1:16–17), and if we want to learn about the way things really and truly are, we must rely on more than the deliverances of nature alone.[196]

Thomas Aquinas's Hermeneutic of Creation

Reading the book of nature in light of the book of scripture is a hermeneutic that is also on display in the thought of Thomas Aquinas.[197] Given its influence on Catholic social teaching, Thomas's thought is an important source for reflecting more deeply on the death of plants and non-human animals in God's creation. Consider this passage from the *Summa Theologiae*:

> Since God is the universal guardian of all that is real, a quality of God's Providence is to allow defects in some particular things so that the complete good of the universe may not be impeded. Were all evils to be denied entrance, many good things would be lacking in the world: there would be no life for the lion were there no animals for its prey, and no patience of martyrs were there no persecution by tyrants. Thus, Augustine says, *Almighty God in no way would permit any evil in his works unless he were not so good and powerful that he could bring good even out of evil.*[198]

In this passage, Thomas affirms God's infinite goodness and power over creation while also acknowledging creaturely death and other evils. Thomas carefully states that God allows these evils rather than wills them because they contribute to the common good. As seen in agroecology, for instance, death brings certain goods into the world that would otherwise be absent – goods on which care of creation as we know it depends. The rule guiding Thomas's hermeneutic is that God would not permit evils unless God could draw good from them (see Gen 50:20). Indeed, it is a mark of God's infinite goodness and power that God works in precisely this way.

Thomas addresses this topic in his discussion of God's providential care for creation. Following Augustine, Thomas views all evil, including the death of plants and non-human animals, as a privation of the good, an absence or lack of being, which is why he speaks of God *allowing, refusing to deny*, and *not preventing* evil, rather than willing it directly as an end.[199] Thomas's moral theological reasoning is therefore not the kind of utilitarian calculus sometimes attributed to him involving, in Southgate's characterization of the same passage, "a balancing of goods and harms, and a theodicy based on the conclusion that

---

[196] See the exchange between Southgate and Messer in Southgate, "God's Creation Wild and Violent, and Our Care for Other Animals," 247; Messer, *Science in Theology*, 84, 93–94.

[197] This discussion leans heavily on Dodds, *Unlocking Divine Action*, 229–258; Davies, *Thomas Aquinas on God and Evil*, 67–70; and Jenkins, *Ecologies of Grace*, 140–148.

[198] Aquinas, *Summa theologiae*, I.22.2 ad 2. Translation slightly altered.

[199] See also Aquinas, *Summa theologiae*, I.19.9 ad 3; *Summa contra Gentiles*, III.1.71.

the goods balance the harms."[200] Against this reading, Thomas is not proposing such a balancing, claiming that the good of lions' existence justifies the harm of antelope death or that the good of martyrs justifies the harm of tyrannical regimes. Nor is he attempting, in the face of these and other natural and moral evils, to vindicate God's goodness and omnipotence. God's goodness and omnipotence are axiomatic to Thomas's whole argument.

Instead, Thomas is offering us a hermeneutic of creation, a way of reading the book of nature in light of God's work in Christ as revealed by scripture. His purpose is to help us better discern creation's goodness and elicit praise of its good and omnipotent Creator. Out of love, Christ willingly endured suffering, death, and crucifixion, bringing good even from these evils. Thomas perceives an analogous pattern characterizing God's work more broadly, including the work of creation: God permits evil, such as antelope death, but without willing it as an end, always directing evil toward the common good. It is God's recreative work in Christ and in the Holy Spirit that reveals this pattern most fully and makes it perceptible to us.

At the same time, Thomas recognizes that the death of plants and non-human animals – what he calls *malum poenae* or evil suffered – is part of the creaturely world as we encounter it. For Thomas, such evil results from God's creation of contingent and mortal creatures – including creatures like us – each of which has integrity, agency, and creativity, and seeks its own flourishing.[201] We remarked on this aspect of natural law in Section 1: that all creatures participate in God's providence by acting as they do, actions that convey the impress of the divine wisdom on them.

Numerous consequences follow from God's creating in this way. One is that contingent and mortal creatures are vulnerable to other creatures' use and to the world at large, leading to suffering and death. A second consequence is that by pursuing their own good, such as providing for themselves and others, creatures must use each other, also resulting in suffering and death. For example, the existence of a biologically rich soil, full of bacteria, fungi, protozoa, nematodes, and worms, involves the death and decomposition of other soil organisms. Similarly, the existence of insects means the consumption of plants and fruits, and the existence of lions involves the hunting of antelopes. Additionally, those that consume may be consumed or die from other causes. In the two consequences just mentioned, we see that the goods of creatures are sometimes rivalrous with one another, and also that death is "created" by creatures, not the Creator. Yet another consequence of God's creating in this manner is that the

---

[200] Southgate, *The Groaning of Creation*, 41–42.
[201] Aquinas, *Summa theologiae*, I.49.2 resp.

goods of particular creatures are intimate with potential privations. Being hunted by lions has, over time, shaped the lives of antelopes, leading to goods like fleetness, long horns, and specialized hooves. Nevertheless, these goods, while intimate with the evils, remain distinct. The vulnerability of such goods does not erase their goodness, nor does it mean they participate any less in God's providence.[202]

Beyond the goods of particular creatures, there are additional goods related to the whole that also arise from God's creating in this way.[203] Without soil, plants, insects, or lions to participate in God's providence and reflect God's goodness in their diverse array, the whole would be diminished by the absence of each creature's unique contribution. The absence of plants would disrupt the conversion of carbon dioxide into oxygen, the absorption of toxins, and the cleaning and filtering of water. The lack of insects would affect pollination and decomposition processes. Without predators like lions, herbivore populations like antelope would overgraze and degrade habitat. Thus, while each creature pursues its good, providing for itself and others, it simultaneously contributes to the good of the whole by being the kind of creature it is and by acting as it does. According to Thomas, God's providential care therefore extends both to particular creatures and to the interconnected whole in which these creatures participate and to which they contribute.[204]

The picture of creation that emerges from Thomas's account is one of a complex, self-sustaining order of interacting creatures, each with its own integrity and agency. According to Thomas, God creates freely and from nothing and therefore did not have to make a world with evils like death. However, such a world would not contain contingent and mortal creatures like ours does. Given the world God did create and in which we live, move, and have our being, evils like death are suffered, while God continually draws good from them. Despite its pervasiveness, then, death remains parasitic. It is an evil that God does not create and that, we hope, will one day be no more.

Once again, Thomas is offering us a hermeneutic of creation, interpreting the book of nature in light of the book of scripture and its revelation of God's love made flesh in Christ.[205] This hermeneutic "tutor[s] charity in perceiving the

---

[202] Jenkins, *Ecologies of Grace*, 146.
[203] See Cory, "Masters, Parasites, or Gardeners?"
[204] Aquinas, *Summa theologiae*, I.48.2 ad 3.
[205] Thomas's is not the only way to read the book of nature without attributing death and other privations to a good and omnipotent God. Thomas's position is subtle. While he does not think that God creates death, he also does not think non-human creaturely death results from the fall. Others do. Griffiths, for instance, follows Augustine in indexing death to the angelic fall (*Decreation*, 131–135). Grey makes similar points (*Theology, Science, and Life*, 219–232). For his part, Sergius Bulgakov offers a meta-historical narration of the human fall, characterizing the Edenic state as an aeon distinct from empirical history as we know it (*Bride of the Lamb*,

lovable," in the words of Willis Jenkins.[206] While not ignoring or minimizing the evil or extent of death, Thomas refuses to grant it and other related evils ontological purchase or regard them as hermeneutically determinative. Instead, he has faith in a good and omnipotent Creator and the law of love as operative throughout creation. With Thomas, we can say that it is a mark of the goodness and power of this love that it brings good even out of evil, including the manifold goods of ecosystems and the ecological principles and processes that enable and sustain creaturely life on earth. In this way, Thomas's hermeneutic of creation allows us to receive and integrate insights from disciplines like agroecology while still maintaining that, in Charles Mathewes's words, "the basic character of the world is found in a love that cannot be explained from the perspective of the world."[207] While in the order of our experience and knowledge of the world, life depends on death, in the order of God's creation and recreation of all things in Christ and the Holy Spirit, the reality is, mysteriously, otherwise.

From this vantage point, the death of other creatures can be viewed with ambivalence. While with Grey, we can experience "distress at the innocent suffering of animals, the waste and destruction wrought by nature's multiple upheavals," recognizing within ourselves "the moral solidarity of the living."[208] We can lament death as an evil unwilled by God, which by faith we believe will one day be no more, because Christ defeated it (Gen 1:29–30; Isa 11:6–9; 1 Cor 15:26–28, 55; Rev 21:4). However, we can also acknowledge that, until that day, and during our pilgrimage on this earth, we must receive death as a gift, albeit one laced with lament. But receive it we must, because, during this pilgrimage, life is inescapably the gift of death. The Creator may not need creation or depend on it, but we do. Our provisioning cannot be disentangled from the death of other creatures, whether of microorganisms, insects, plants, or other animals.

The right response to this reality is not to ignore, deny, or flee from its difficulty, but to receive it with humility, give thanks to the good and omnipotent God who brings good from death, and look in hope toward the day when death will finally be no more. In light of scripture and its testimony to the true source of all created life, death even becomes a site where we can glimpse, as if through

---

164–119). Deane-Drummond elaborates on the ecological implications of Bulgakov's account in numerous works, including *Shadow Sophia*. Yet another approach is Messer's Barthian reading of the problem of natural evil as not corresponding with God's original creation (*Science in Theology*, 88–93).

[206] Jenkins, *Ecologies of Grace*, 145.   [207] Mathewes, *Evil and the Augustinian Tradition*, 237.

[208] Grey, *Theology, Science, and Life*, 231. To be clear, the suggestion here is not that Thomas himself would endorse such distress, but rather that those who wish to think in line with his teachings can.

a broken mirror, the Paschal mystery of Christ, the one who, like a seed, falls to the ground and dies, and in dying, brings abundant life (Jn 12:23–26).

A Theologically-Engaged Agroecology

This Element, as an exercise in a form of science-engaged theology, has primarily focused on agroecology's contribution to Catholic social teaching. Its main purpose has been to demonstrate how agroecology aids those committed to social teaching in better tilling and keeping the earth, while also illuminating agroecology's theological significance and its potential to clarify and deepen a natural law ethic. In essence, agroecology has a crucial role to play in developing an ecology capable of remedying the damage we have done to our common home. However, in a dialogue of wisdom, the learning is not simply unidirectional. All interlocutors should be open to receiving wisdom from others and to the possibility of transformation. Therefore, can more be said about Catholic social teaching's contribution to the dialogue and what disciplines like agroecology might learn from it?

One of Catholic social teaching's key contributions, as evident throughout this Element, pertains to linguistic and conceptual implications deriving from the doctrine of creation. In these pages, my engagement with agroecology has relied most basically on the language of creation, rather than terms like nature, the environment, or even ecology, to describe the bonds uniting human creatures with the world. Following the guidance of *Laudato si'*, I have used these latter terms while also reshaping them in light of the doctrine of creation and the three fundamental relationships of human life. The rationale for this approach is not to dismiss the concerns of agroecologists but to display to them the implications of engaging with Catholic social teaching. It is also to demonstrate how recasting agroecology in this manner can expand the discipline of agroecology, pushing it in new directions.[209]

Catholic social teaching can also contribute to the dialogue of wisdoms by surfacing the kind of moral reasoning agroecologists often employ but seldom explicitly reflect on.[210] We have seen how agroecology's ecological grammar functions both descriptively and normatively, raising questions about our understanding of the creation, the kinds of creatures we are, and our purpose on this earth. This form of moral reasoning, I have argued, has important affinities with natural law. Yet, agroecology rarely reflects on the cosmological, anthropological, and ethical questions raised by the discipline. What does it mean to be human, and how should we live? Are we, as Therese Cory asks,

---

[209] Grey makes a similar point about the life sciences in *Theology, Science, and Life* (see 216).
[210] Whelan, "Agroecology and Natural Law"; Whelan, "Agroecology's Moral Vision."

masters of nature, parasites on it, or gardeners meant to till and keep it?[211] What kind of world do we want to leave to those who will come after us and who will also depend on it? As Francis notes in *Laudato si'*, "Unless we struggle with these deeper issues, I do not believe that our concern for ecology will produce significant results" (no. 160). Moral theological traditions like Catholic social teaching can serve as important sources of wisdom as agroecologists explore these important but insufficiently examined questions.[212]

As we have already seen, one of these questions relates to the kinds of creatures we are and even to the issue of human distinctiveness, the acknowledgment of which cuts against powerful currents in ecological theology and ethics today. For instance, Lynn White influentially argues that the ecological crisis results from "the Christian dogma of man's [sic] transcendence of, and rightful mastery over, nature."[213] In response to this charge of anthropocentrism and instrumentalism of nature, many theologians and ethicists have sought to recover an ecological worldview centered on the naturalness of the human creature, its embeddedness in creation, and the inherent value of the wider creaturely world. Once again, while scholars have rightly contested White's argument and its legacy, the concern here is not whether his diagnosis is correct but rather the effect that diagnosis has had on ecological theologians and ethicists, and whether their response is adequate to the kinds of creatures we are.

This concern manifests itself in the conflicting responses of agroecology and industrial agriculture to the questions raised earlier about cosmology, anthropology, and ethics. These conflicts and the divergent responses reveal that we are creatures capable of discerning or disregarding an ecological grammar. Even once discerned, we can decide whether to adhere to it. Similarly, we can acknowledge our dependencies on other creatures or live thoughtlessly at their expense. We can till and keep the earth or maximize production and extract. We can accept or reject God's providential care for creation as a law for our lives, just as we can accept or reject our existence and that of the creation as a gift of the Creator. In these divergent responses, we face the mystery of human freedom and the choice, from the perspective of social teaching, to become either truer or falser to the creatures we are and the creation we share.

In this way, agroecology's own terms reveal us to be creatures that are simultaneously inside and outside the ecological grammar that the discipline discerns and on which it bases agriculture. We are inside because we are

---

[211] Cory, "Masters, Parasites, or Gardeners?"

[212] It is possible for people to grasp the natural law and put it into practice without giving a theoretical account of the natural law or reflecting on its foundations in God. ITC, *In Search of a Universal Ethic*, sec. 3.1.60.

[213] White, "The Historical Roots of Our Ecologic Crisis," 1206.

embodied creatures. We come from the earth and return to it, depending on other creatures and ecological principles and processes as we live in flesh. But we are also, in a sense, outside that grammar, because the decision regarding which of these divergent paths to follow is a matter of human freedom and how we decide to use it. Whether or not we will integrate a responsiveness to the principles, rules, and laws of ecological systems into the principles, rules, and laws that order our lives and societies remains an open question.

In her exploration of the mysterious status of the human creature, Grey writes that "an agricultural future worthy of human beings needs a metaphysics which takes human earthliness seriously but does not absolutize it." She continues: "Farming takes place in that space of ambivalence; a fraught complicity with a necessary violence, an answerability to nature that at the same time demands that we recognize our unlikeness to other creatures. . . . We need a language for this unnatural-ness of humans, as well as our naturalness."[214] Currently, agroecology has yet to develop a language for this "unnatural-ness." However, a moral theological tradition like Catholic social teaching already has one ready to hand. It is that, in addition to being dust that will return to dust, we are also dust inbreathed by God and ultimately destined for heaven.[215]

It is especially on this terrain that moral theological traditions like Catholic social teaching have much to contribute to the dialogue of wisdoms agroecology proposes. Social teaching not only acknowledges the reality and implications of human freedom but also diagnoses the deepest source of the damage we have done to our common home: the abuse of freedom that the tradition calls sin. According to Francis, the presumption of human creatures to prescind from their creaturely status and usurp the place of God has led the three fundamental relationships that ground human life to go radically awry, pitting human life against the planet's. "Our Sister, Mother Earth, who sustains and governs us," he begins *Laudato si'*, "now cries out to us because of the harm we have inflicted on her by our irresponsible use and abuse of the goods with which God has endowed her. We have come to see ourselves as her lords and masters, entitled to plunder her at will" (nos. 1–2).

Lording over, mastering, and plundering – all of these bear the marks of sin. Those who behave in this way have forgotten perhaps the most fundamental truth about the human creature: that, in Francis's words, "we are not God" (no. 67) but creatures brought into being by the Creator. Our bodies are of the earth, and our lives, like those of other embodied creatures, determine the earth's use. Because we are embodied, the damage sin does to the interior landscape of our lives necessarily impinges on external landscapes, damaging

---

[214] Grey, "The Metaphysics of Farming." [215] Hütter, *Dust Bound for Heaven*.

soil, water, air, and the lives of other creatures in the process (no. 2). Similarly, those who act as lords, masters, and plunderers have also forgotten that the earth is God's, not ours (Ps 24:1, Dt 10:14, Lev 25:23), and that our vocation on the earth is to be tillers and keepers of a gift God has given for common use. It is our duty to provide for ourselves and for one another from the earth's bounty, ensuring that all people have access to it, while also preserving the gift's ongoing fruitfulness for those who will follow us (no. 67). All of this, Francis remarks, is a matter of fidelity to the Creator (no. 93).

"A spirituality which forgets God as all-powerful and Creator is not acceptable," Francis warns us. "That is how we end up worshiping earthly powers, or ourselves usurping the place of God, even to the point of claiming an unlimited right to trample his creation underfoot" (no. 75). Fittingly, at the center of *Laudato si'* is Francis's call for a spirituality – God's graceful transformation of our interior landscape – that can inspire an ecological conversion, whereby the effects of the encounter with Christ change our relation to the world and its creatures (nos. 75, 216–221).[216] As Francis observes elsewhere, the deepest source of such a spirituality is receptivity to "the Lord, who is the first to care for us, [and] teaches us to care for our brothers and sisters and the environment which he daily gives us." "This," he continues, "is the first ecology that we need."[217] Our need for this first and most fundamental ecology is why agroecology's dialogue of wisdoms has much to gain from engaging with moral theological traditions like Catholic social teaching.

---

[216] On this point, see also Wirzba, *Agrarian Spirit*.
[217] Francis, *Querida amazonia*, no. 41.

Bibliography

Agriculture and Economic Development Analysis Division. *The State of Food and Agriculture (2014): Innovation in Family Farming.* Rome: FAO, 2014.

Albertson, David, and Cabell King, eds. *Without Nature? A New Condition for Theology.* New York: Fordham University Press, 2009.

Altieri, Miguel. *Agroecology: The Science of Sustainable Agriculture.* Boulder, CO: Westview Press, 1995.

Altieri, Miguel A. "Linking Ecologists and Traditional Farmers in the Search for Sustainable Agriculture." *Frontiers in Ecology and the Environment* 2, no. 1 (2004): 35–42.

"Why Study Traditional Agriculture?" In C. R. Carroll, J. H. Vandermeer, & P. Rossett (eds.), *Agroecology* (pp. 551–564). New York: McGraw-Hill, 1990.

Ambrose of Milan. "On Naboth." In Boniface Ramsey (ed.), *Ambrose* (pp. 117–144). New York: Routledge, 1997.

Aquinas, Thomas. *Summa Contra Gentiles.* Notre Dame: University of Notre Dame Press, 1956.

Summa Theologiae, Vol. 2. Cambridge: Cambridge University Press, 2006.
Summa Theologiae, Vol. 5. Cambridge: Cambridge University Press, 2006.
Summa Theologiae, Vol. 8. Cambridge: Cambridge University Press, 2006.
Summa Theologiae, Vol. 13. Cambridge: Cambridge University Press, 2006.
Summa Theologiae, Vol. 28. Cambridge: Cambridge University Press, 2006.

Aristotle. *Physics: The Complete Works of Aristotle.* Princeton, NJ: Princeton University Press, 1984.

Augustine, *The Confessions.* Translated by Maria Boulding. New York: New City Press, 2001.

Avery, Dennis T. *Saving the World with Pesticides and Plastics.* Washington, DC: Hudson Institute, 2000.

Balmford, Andrew, Tatsuya Amano, Harriet Bartlett, et al. "The Environmental Costs and Benefits of High-Yield Farming." *Nature Sustainability* 1, no. 9 (2018): 477–485.

Barker, Eugene, ed. "Thomas M. Duke to Stephen F. Austin, 06-Xx-1824." In *Annual Report of the American Historical Association for the Year 1919: The Austin Papers*, Vol. 1. Washington, DC: Government Printing Office, 1924, pp. 842–843.

Benedict XVI. "Address to the Participants in the International Congress on Natural Moral Law." Clementine Hall, February 12, 2007.

———. *Caritas in Veritate*. Encyclical Letter. June 29, 2009. www.vatican.va.

Benkeblia, Noureddine, ed. *Climate Change and Crop Production: Foundations for Agroecosystem Resilience*. Boca Raton, FL: CRC Press, 2019.

Bensin, Basil. M. "Possibilities for International Cooperation in Agroecology Investigation." *International Review of Agriculture* 21 (1930): 277–289.

Berry, Wendell. *The Poetry of William Carlos Williams of Rutherford*. Berkley, CA: Counterpoint Press, 2011.

———. *The Unsettling of America*. New York: Counterpoint Press, 2015.

Botelho, Maria Izabel Vieira, Irene Maria Cardoso, and Kei Otsuki. "'I Made a Pact with God, with Nature, and with Myself': Exploring Deep Agroecology." *Agroecology and Sustainable Food Systems* 40, no. 2 (February 7, 2016): 116–131.

Brown, Peter. *Through the Eye of a Needle: Wealth, the Fall of Rome, and the Making of Christianity in the West, 350–550 AD*. Princeton, NJ: Princeton University Press, 2012.

Bulgakov, Sergius. *The Bride of the Lamb*. Translated by Boris Jakim. Grand Rapids, MI: Wm. B. Eerdmans-Lightning Source, 2001.

Cahill, Lisa Sowle. *Global Justice, Christology, and Christian Ethics*. Cambridge: Cambridge University Press, 2013.

Calderón, Claudia Irene, Claudia Jerónimo, Alexandra Praun, et al. "Agroecology-Based Farming Provides Grounds for More Resilient Livelihoods among Smallholders in Western Guatemala." *Agroecology and Sustainable Food Systems* 42, no. 10 (November 26, 2018): 1128–1169.

Campbell, Bruce M., Jason Hall-Spencer, John Ingram, Navin Ramankutty, and Drew Shindell. "Agriculture Production as a Major Driver of the Earth System Exceeding Planetary Boundaries." *Ecology and Society* 22, no. 4 (2017).

Carroll, Roland C. John H. Vandermeer, Peter M. Rosset, eds. *Agroecology*. New York: McGraw-Hill Book, 1990.

Carson, Rachel. *Silent Spring*. New York: Houghton Mifflin Harcourt, 1962.

Cavanaugh, William T., and James K. A. Smith, eds. *Evolution and the Fall*. Grand Rapids, MI: Wm. B. Eerdmans, 2017.

Chambers, Robert. *Whose Reality Counts? Putting the First Last*. London: Intermediate Technology, 1997.

Chapman, Brian R., and Eric G. Boen. *The Natural History of Texas*. College Station, TX: Texas A&M University Press, 2018.

Cory, Therese. "Masters, Parasites, or Gardeners? Thomistic Reflections on Environmental Ethics." Presented at the Thomistic Institute, Baylor University, January 31, 2018.

Crews, Timothy E., and Douglas J. Cattani. "Strategies, Advances, and Challenges in Breeding Perennial Grain Crops." *Sustainability* 10, no. 7 (2018): 2192.

Crutzen, Paul J., and Eugene F. Stoermer. "The Anthropocene." *IGBP Newsletter* 41, no. 1 (2000): 17–18.

Curry, Helen Anne. "Breeding Uniformity and Banking Diversity: The Genescapes of Industrial Agriculture, 1935–1970." *Global Environment* 10, no. 1 (2017): 83–113.

Davies, Brian. *Thomas Aquinas on God and Evil*. New York: Oxford University Press, 2011.

Davison, Andrew. "Science and Specificity: Interdisciplinary Teaching between Theology, Religion, and the Natural Sciences." *Zygon* 57, no. 1 (2022): 233–243.

Deane-Drummond, Celia. "Joining in the Dance: Catholic Social Teaching and Ecology." *New Blackfriars* 93, no. 1044 (2012): 193–212.

"Laudato si and the Natural Sciences: An Assessment of Possibilities and Limits." *Theological Studies* 77, no. 2 (2016): 392–415.

Deane-Drummond, Celia E. *Shadow Sophia: Evolution of Wisdom*, Vol. 2. Oxford: Oxford University Press, 2021.

"Declaration of the International Forum for Agroecology, Nyéléni, Mali." *Development* 58 (2015): 163–168.

Descola, Philippe. *Beyond Nature and Culture*. Chicago: University of Chicago Press, 2013.

Dodds, Michael. *Unlocking Divine Action*. Washington, DC: Catholic University of America Press, 2012.

Douglas, Heather E. *Science, Policy, and the Value-Free Ideal*. Pittsburgh: University of Pittsburgh Press, 2009.

Dupré, Louis. *Passage to Modernity: An Essay in the Hermeneutics of Nature and Culture*. New Haven, CT: Yale University Press, 1993.

Edwards, Denis. *Jesus the Wisdom of God: An Ecological Theology*. Eugene, OR: Wipf & Stock, 1995.

Ellis, Frank. *Rural Livelihoods and Diversity in Developing Countries*. New York: Oxford University Press, 2000.

Elmqvist, Thomas, Carl Folke, Magnus Nyström, et al. "Response Diversity, Ecosystem Change, and Resilience." *Frontiers in Ecology and the Environment* 1, no. 9 (2003): 488–494.

Federico, Giovanni. *Feeding the World: An Economic History of Agriculture, 1800–2000*. Princeton, NJ: University of Princeton Press, 2005.

Finnis, John. "Aquinas as a Primary Source of Catholic Social Teaching." In G. V. Bradley and E. C. Brugger (eds.), *Catholic Social Teaching: A Volume of Scholarly Essays* (pp. 11–33). Cambridge: Cambridge University Press, 2019.

Fitzgerald, Deborah. *Every Farm a Factory: The Industrial Ideal in American Agriculture*. New Haven, CT: Yale University Press, 2010.

Flyvbjerg, Bent. *Making Social Science Matter: Why Social Inquiry Fails and How It Can Succeed Again*. Translated by Steven Sampson. Cambridge: Cambridge University Press, 2001.

Fonteyne, Simon, José B. Castillo Caamal, Santiago Lopez-Ridaura, et al. "Review of Agronomic Research on the *Milpa*, the Traditional Polyculture System of Mesoamerica." *Frontiers in Agronomy* 5 (2023).

Food and Agricultural Organization (FAO), IFAD, UNICEF, WFP, and WHO. *The State of Food Security and Nutrition in the World 2024 – Financing to End Hunger, Food Insecurity and Malnutrition in All Its Forms*. Rome: FAO, 2024.

Francis I. "Fraternity, the Foundation and Pathway to Peace," January 1, 2014.
  "Address to the Participants in the World Meeting of Popular Movements." Old Synod Hall, Vatican City, October 28, 2014.
  Laudato si'. Encyclical Letter. May 24, 2015.
  "Address to the Participants in the Second World Meeting of Popular Movements." Expo Feria Exhibition Center, Santa Cruz de la Sierra, Bolivia, July 9, 2015.
  "Address to the Participants in the Third World Meeting of Popular Movements." Paul VI Audience Hall, November 5, 2016.
  Querida Amazonia. Post-Synodal Apostolic Exhortation. February 2, 2020.
  Let Us Dream: The Path to a Better Future. New York: Simon & Schuster, 2022.

Francis of Assisi. "Canticle of the Creatures." In R. J. Armstrong, J. A. Wayne Hellmann, and W. J. Short (eds.), *Early Documents*, Vol. 1 (pp. 113-114). New York: New City Press, 2001.

Freire, Paulo. *Extensión o Comunicación? La Concientización En El Medio Rural*. México: Siglo Veintiuno Editores, 1973.

French, William. "With Radical Amazement: Ecology and the Recovery of Creation." In D. Albertson (ed.), *Without Nature? A New Condition for Theology* (pp. 54–79). Fordham University Press, 2010.

French, William C. "Natural Law and Ecological Responsibility: Drawing on the Thomistic Tradition." *University of St. Thomas Law Journal* 5, no. 1 (2008): 12–36.

Friesen, Carl A. "Theological Foundations for a Christian Land Ethic." PhD, Notre Dame, 2023.

Fussell, Betty. "Translating Maize into Corn: The Transformation of America's Native Grain." *Social Research* 66, no. 1 (1999): 41–65.

Gardner, Sarah M., Stephen J. Ramsden, and Rosemary S. Hails. *Agricultural Resilience: Perspectives from Ecology and Economics*. Cambridge: Cambridge University Press, 2019.

Garibaldi, Lucas A., Georg K. S. Andersson, Fabrice Requier, et al. "Complementarity and Synergisms among Ecosystem Services Supporting Crop Yield." *Global Food Security* 17 (2018): 38–47.

Giraldo, Omar Felipe. *Ecología Política de la Agricultura: Agroecología y Posdesarrollo*. México: El Colegio de la Frontera Sur, 2018.

Gliessman, Stephen R., V. Ernesto Méndez, Victor M. Izzo, Eric W. Engles, and Andrew Gerlicz. *Agroecology: Leading the Transformation to a Just and Sustainable Food System*. 4th ed. Boca Raton, FL: CRC Press, 2023.

Gliessman, Stephen R. "Defining Agroecology." *Agroecology and Sustainable Food Systems* 42, no. 6 (2018): 599–600.

Gonzalez, Andrew, and Michel Loreau. "The Causes and Consequences of Compensatory Dynamics in Ecological Communities." *Annual Review of Ecology, Evolution, and Systematics* 40, no. 1 (2009): 393–414.

Goodman, David, Bernardo Sorj, and John Wilkinson. *From Farming to Biotechnology: A Theory of Agro-Industrial Development*. New York: Basil Blackwell, 1987.

Grey, Carmody. "The Only Creature God Willed for Its Own Sake': Anthropocentrism in *Laudato si'* and *Gaudium et Spes*." *Modern Theology* 36, no. 4 (2020): 865–883.

"A Theologian's Perspective on Science-Engaged Theology." *Modern Theology* 37, no. 2 (2021): 489–494.

"The Metaphysics of Farming." Presented at *Contestations in Land and Agriculture: Contestations in Land and Agriculture: New Perspectives in Theology and Ethics*. Christ Church, Oxford University, May 15, 2022.

Theology, Science and Life. New York: T&T Clark, 2024.

Griffiths, Paul J. *Decreation: The Last Things of All Creatures*. Waco, TX: Baylor University Press, 2014.

Groppe, Elizabeth. "The Way of Wisdom: 'Keep Hold of Instruction; Do Not Let Go; Guard Her, for She Is Your Life' (Prov 3:14)." In T. Winwright & J. Schaefer (eds.), *Environmental Justice and Climate Change: Assessing Pope Benedict XVI's Ecological Vision for the Catholic Church in the United States* (pp. 127–148). New York: Lexington Books, 2013.

Haraway, Donna. "Anthropocene, Capitalocene, Plantationocene, Chthulucene: Making Kin." *Environmental Humanities* 6, no. 1 (2015): 159–165.

Harrison, Peter. *The Bible, Protestantism, and the Rise of Natural Science.* New York: Cambridge University Press, 2001.

Hecht, Susannah B. "The Evolution of Agroecological Thought." In *Agroecology: The Science of Sustainable Agriculture* (pp. 1–19). Boulder, CO: Westview Press, 1995.

Heinemann, Jack A., Melanie Massaro, Dorien S. Coray, Sarah Zanon Agapito-Tenfen, and Jiajun Dale Wen. "Sustainability and Innovation in Staple Crop Production in the US Midwest." *International Journal of Agricultural Sustainability* 12, no. 1 (2014): 71–88.

Hendrickson, Mary K., Philip H. Howard, Emily M. Miller, and Douglas H. Constance. "The Food System: Concentration and Its Impacts." Family Farm Action Alliance, November 19, 2020.

Henke, Christopher R. *Cultivating Science, Harvesting Power: Science and Industrial Agriculture in California.* Cambridge, MA: The MIT Press, 2008.

Hernández Castillo, R. Aída. "Organic Growers: Agroecological Catholicism and the Invention of Traditions." In *Histories and Stories from Chiapas: Border Identities in Southern Mexico* (pp. 161–186). Austin, TX: University of Texas Press, 2001.

Hernández Xoloctozi, Efraím. *Xolocotzia: Obras de Efraím Hernández Xolocotzi.* Texcoco: Universidad Autónoma Chapingo, 2014.

Hibbs, Thomas S. *A Theology of Creation: Ecology, Art, and Laudato si'.* Notre Dame: University of Notre Dame Press, 2023.

Higgs, Eric. *Nature by Design: People, Natural Processes, and Ecological Restoration.* Cambridge, MA: The MIT Press, 2003.

High Level Panel of Experts on Food Security and Nutrition. "Agroecological and Other Innovative Approaches for Sustainable Agriculture and Food Systems That Enhance Food Security and Nutrition." A Report by the High Level Panel of Experts on Food Security and Nutrition. Rome: Committee on World Food Security, 2019.

Hittinger, Russell. "The Situation of Natural Law in Catholic Theology." In J. Berkman and W. C. Mattison III (eds.), *Searching for a Universal Ethic: Multidiciplinary, Eceumenical, and Interfaith Responses to the Catholic Natural Law Tradition* (pp. 111–122). Grand Rapids, MI: Wm. B. Eerdmans, 2014.

Holling, Crawford. S. "Resilience and Stability of Ecological Systems." *Annual Review of Ecology and Systematics* 4, no. 1 (1973): 1–23.

Holt-Giménez, Eric. "Measuring Farmers Agroecological Resistance after Hurricane Mitch in Nicaragua: A Case Study in Participatory, Sustainable Land Management Impact Monitoring." *Agriculture, Ecosystems & Environment* 93, no. 1 (2002): 87–105.

Hugh of Saint-Victor. *De tribus diebus*. ed. Dominique Poirel. Turnhout: Brepols, 2002.

Hütter, Reinhard. *Dust Bound for Heaven: Explorations in the Theology of Thomas Aquinas*. Grand Rapids, MI: Wm. B. Eerdmans, 2012.

Intergovernmental Panel on Climate Change. *Climate Change and Land: An IPCC Special Report on Climate Change, Desertification, Land Degradation, Sustainable Land Management, Food Security, and Greenhouse Gas Fluxes in Terrestrial Ecosystems*. Intergovernmental Panel on Climate Change, 2019.

International Assessment of Agricultural Knowledge, Science, and Technology for Development. *Agriculture at a Crossroads: The Global Report*. Washington, DC: Island Press, 2009.

International Panel of Experts on Sustainable Food Systems. "From Uniformity to Diversity: A Paradigm Shift from Industrial Agriculture to Diversified Agroecological Systems." Louvain-la-Neuve: International Panel of Experts on Sustainable Food Systems, 2016.

International Theological Commission. *In Search of a Universal Ethic: A New Look at the Natural Law*, 2009. www.vatican.va

Jackson, Wes. *New Roots for Agriculture*. Lincoln, NE: University of Nebraska Press, 1980.

Jenkins, Willis. "Biodiversity and Salvation: Thomistic Roots for Environmental Ethics." *The Journal of Religion* 83, no. 3 (2003): 401–420.

Ecologies of Grace: Environmental Ethics and Christian Theology. New York: Oxford University Press, 2008.

"After Lynn White: Religious Ethics and Environmental Problems." *The Journal of Religious Ethics* 37, no. 2 (2009): 283–309.

John Paul II. *Sollicitudo Rei Socialis*. Encyclical Letter. December 30, 1987.

Centesimus Annus. Encyclical Letter. May 1, 1991.

Johnson, Elizabeth A. *Ask the Beasts: Darwin and the God of Life*. New York: Bloomsbury USA, 2014.

Khoury, Colin K., Stephen Brush, Denise E. Costich, et al. "Crop Genetic Erosion: Understanding and Responding to Loss of Crop Diversity." *The New Phytologist* 233, no. 1 (2022): 84–118.

Kimmerer, Robin Wall. *Braiding Sweetgrass: Indigenous Wisdom, Scientific Knowledge, and the Teachings of Plants*. Minneapolis, MN: Milkweed Editions, 2015.

Kloppenburg, Jack Ralph. *First the Seed: The Political Economy of Plant Biotechnology (1492–2000)*. Cambridge: Cambridge University Press, 1988.

Koohafkan, Parviz, and Miguel Altieri. *Globally Important Agricultural Heritage Systems: A Legacy for the Future*. Rome: Food and Agriculture Organization of the United Nations, 2011.

Kremen, Claire, and Albie Miles. "Ecosystem Services in Biologically Diversified versus Conventional Farming Systems: Benefits, Externalities, and Trade-Offs." *Ecology and Society* 17, no. 4 (2012): 40.

Lacey, Hugh. *Values and Objectivity in Science: The Current Controversy about Transgenic Crops*. Lanham, MD: Lexington Books, 2005.

Lappé, Frances Moore, and Joseph Collins. *World Hunger: Ten Myths*. New York: Grove Press, 2015.

Latour, Bruno. *We Have Never Been Modern*. Cambridge, MA: Harvard University Press, 1993.

Laudato si' Movement. October 12, 2023.

Liebman, Matt, and Lisa Schulte. "Enhancing Agroecosystem Performance and Resilience through Increased Diversification of Landscapes and Cropping Systems." *Elementa: Science of the Anthropocene* 3 (2015): 000041.

Lin, Brenda B. "Agroforestry Management as an Adaptive Strategy against Potential Microclimate Extremes in Coffee Agriculture." *Agricultural and Forest Meteorology* 144, no. 1 (2007): 85–94.

———. "Resilience in Agriculture through Crop Diversification: Adaptive Management for Environmental Change." *BioScience* 61, no. 3 (2011): 183–193.

Lin, Brenda B., Ivette Perfecto, and John Vandermeer. "Synergies between Agricultural Intensification and Climate Change Could Create Surprising Vulnerabilities for Crops." *BioScience* 58, no. 9 (2008): 847–854.

Linzey, Andrew, and Dorothy Yamamoto, eds. "Are Animals Fallen?" In *Animals on the Agenda: Questions about Animals for Theology and Ethics* (147–160). London: SCM Press, 1998.

Lloyd, Michael. "The Humanity of Fallenness." In T. Bradshaw (ed.), *Grace and Truth in the Secular Age* (pp. 66–82). Grand Rapids, MI: Eerdmans, 1998.

Lodge, David M., ed. *Religion and the New Ecology: Environmental Responsibility in a World in Flux*. 1st ed. Notre Dame: University of Notre Dame Press, 2006.

Lowder, Sarah K., Marco V. Sánchez, and Raffaele Bertini. "Which Farms Feed the World and Has Farmland Become More Concentrated?" *World Development* 142 (2021): 105455.

Malm, Andreas, and Alf Hornborg. "The Geology of Mankind? A Critique of the Anthropocene Narrative." *The Anthropocene Review* 1, no. 1 (2014): 62–69.

Martínez-Torres, María Elena, and Peter M. Rosset. "Diálogo de Saberes in La Vía Campesina: Food Sovereignty and Agroecology." *The Journal of Peasant Studies* 41, no. 6 (2021): 979–997.

Mathewes, Charles T. *Evil and the Augustinian Tradition*. New York: Cambridge University Press, 2001.

May, Robert M. *Stability and Complexity in Model Ecosystems*. Princeton, NJ: Princeton University Press, 2001.

Mazoyer, Marcel, and Laurence Roudart. *A History of World Agriculture: From the Neolithic Age to the Current Crisis*. New York: Monthly Review Press, 2006.

McCabe, Herbert. "The Myth of God Incarnate." *New Blackfriars* 58, no. 687 (1977): 350–57.

Merchant, Carolyn. *The Death of Nature: Women, Ecology, and the Scientific Revolution*. New York: HarperOne, 1990.

Messer, Neil. *Flourishing: Health, Disease, and Bioethics in Theological Perspective*. Grand Rapids, MI: Wm. B. Eerdmans, 2013.

Science in Theology: Encounters between Science and the Christian Tradition. New York: T&T Clark, 2020.

Mier y Terán Giménez Cacho, Mateo, Omar Felipe Giraldo, Miriam Aldasoro, et al. "Bringing Agroecology to Scale: Key Drivers and Emblematic Cases." *Agroecology and Sustainable Food Systems* 42, no. 6 (2018): 637–665.

Millennium Ecosystem Assessment. *Ecosystems and Human Well-Being: Synthesis*. Washington, DC: Island Press, 2005.

Montgomery, David. *Growing a Revolution: Bringing Our Soil Back to Life*. New York: W. W. Norton, 2018.

Morales, Helda. "Pest Management in Traditional Tropical Ecosystems: Lessons for Pest Prevention Research and Extension." *Integrated Pest Management Reviews* 7 (2002): 145–163.

Morales, Helda, and Ivette Perfecto. "Traditional Knowledge and Pest Management in the Guatemalan Highlands." *Agricultural and Human Values* 17 (2000): 49–63.

Mt. Pleasant, Jane. "Food Yields and Nutrient Analyses of the Three Sisters: A Haudenosaunee Cropping System." *Ethnobiology Letters* 7, no. 1 (2016): 87–98.

Nabhan, Gary Paul. *The Desert Smells Like Rain*. San Francisco, CA: North Point Press, 1982.

Gathering the Desert. Tucson, AZ: University of Arizona Press, 1985.

Nash, James A. "Seeking Moral Norms in Nature: Natural Law and Ecological Responsibility." In D. T. Hessel and R. Radford Ruether (eds.), *Christianity and Ecology* (pp. 227–250). Cambridge: Harvard University Press, 2000.

Neeson, J. M. *Commoners: Common Right, Enclosure and Social Change in England, 1700–1820*. Cambridge: Cambridge University Press, 1996.

Nicholls, Clara I., Miguel A. Altieri, and Luis Vazquez. "Agroecological Principles for the Conversion of Farming Systems." In *Agroecological Practices for Sustainable Agriculture: Principles, Applications, and Making the Transition*. New Jersey, NJ: World Scientific Europe, 2017.

Nolte, Kerstin, Wytske Chamberlain, and Markus Giger. *International Land Deals for Agriculture: Fresh Insights from the Land Matrix: Analytical Report II*. Bern: Bern Open, 2016.

Northcott, Michael S. *The Environment and Christian Ethics*. New York: Cambridge University Press, 1996.

Northgaard, Richard B., and Thomas O. Sikor. "The Methodology and Practice of Agroecology." In *Agroecology: The Science of Sustainable Agriculture*. Boulder, CO: Westview Press, 1995.

Parham, John. *Green Man Hopkins: Poetry and the Victorian Ecological Imagination*. Leiden: Brill, 2010.

Pendergrast, Mark. *Uncommon Grounds: The History of Coffee and How It Transformed Our World*. New York: Basic Books, 2019.

Perfecto, Ivette, and John Vandermeer. "The Agroecological Matrix as Alternative to the Land-Sparing/Agriculture Intensification Model." *Proceedings of the National Academy of Sciences* 107, no. 13 (2010): 5786–5791.

Perfecto, Ivette, John Vandermeer, and Angus Wright. *Nature's Matrix: Linking Agriculture, Biodiversity Conservation and Food Sovereignty*. Sterling, VA: Earthscan, 2009.

Perry, John, and Joanna Leidenhag. "What Is Science-Engaged Theology?" *Modern Theology* 37, no. 2 (2021): 245–253.

——— *Science-Engaged Theology*. Cambridge: Cambridge University Press, 2023.

Petraitis, Peter. *Multiple Stable States in Natural Ecosystems*. New York: Oxford University Press, 2013.

Phalan, Ben, Rhys E. Green, Lynn V. Dicks, et al. "How Can Higher-Yield Farming Help to Spare Nature?" *Science* 351, no. 6272 (2016): 450–451.

Philpott, Stacy M., Brenda B. Lin, Shalene Jha, and Shannon J. Brines. "A Multi-Scale Assessment of Hurricane Impacts on Agricultural Landscapes

Based on Land Use and Topographic Features." *Agriculture, Ecosystems & Environment* 128, no. 1 (2008): 12–20.

Pope, Stephen J. "Natural Law in Catholic Social Teaching." In K. R. Himes (ed.), *Modern Catholic Social Teaching: Commentaries and Interpretations* (pp. 41–71). Washington, DC: Georgetown University Press, 2018.

Porter, Jean. *Natural and Divine Law: Reclaiming the Tradition for Christian Ethics*. Grand Rapids, MI: Wm. B. Eerdmans, 1999.

Nature as Reason: A Thomistic Theory of the Natural Law. Grand Rapids, MI: William B. Eerdmans, 2005.

Reijntjes, Coen, Bertus Haverkort, and Ann Waters-Bayer. *Farming for the Future: An Introduction to Low-External Input and Sustainable Agriculture*. Leusden: ILEIA, 1992.

Reyes, Liam de los. "By Nature Common: Foundations for a Natural Law Theory of the Convention of Property." PhD, Notre Dame, 2021.

Ricciardi, Vincent, Navin Ramankutty, Zia Mehrabi, Larissa Jarvis, and Brenton Chookolingo. "How Much of the World's Food Do Smallholders Produce?" *Global Food Security* 17 (2018): 64–72.

Ritchie, Hannah. *Not the End of the World: How We Can Be the First Generation to Build a Sustainable Planet*. New York: Little, Brown Spark, 2024.

Ritchie, Hannah, and Max Roser. "Urbanization," 2018. https://ourworldindata.org/urbanization.

Rockström, Johan, Will Steffen, Kevin Noone, et al. "A Safe Operating Space for Humanity." *Nature* 461, no. 7263 (2009): 472–475.

Rolston III, Holmes. "Naturalizing and Systematizing Evil." In W. B. Drees (ed.), *Is Nature Ever Evil?* (pp. 67–86). New York: Routledge, 2003.

Romero, Óscar A. *Homilías*, Vol. IV. San Salvador: UCA Editores, 2007.

Rosset, Peter M., and Miguel A. Altieri. "Agroecology versus Input Substitution: A Fundamental Contradiction of Sustainable Agriculture." *Society & Natural Resources* 10, no. 3 (1997): 283–295.

Russell, A. Wendy, Fern Wickson, and Anna L. Carew. "Transdisciplinarity: Context, Contradictions, and Capacity." *Futures* 40, no. 5 (2008): 460–472.

Russell, Edmund. *War and Nature: Fighting Humans and Insects with Chemicals from World War I to Silent Spring*. New York: Cambridge University Press, 2001.

Schutter, Olivier de. "Access to Land and the Right to Food." Presented at the 65th General Assembly of the United Nations [A/65/281]. Geneva: Human Rights Council, October 21, 2010.

"Agroecology and the Right to Food." Report presented at the 16th Session of the United Nations Human Rights Council [A/HRC/16/49]. Geneva: Human Rights Council, December 11, 2010.

Scott, James C. *Seeing like a State: How Certain Schemes to Improve the Human Condition Have Failed.* New Haven, CT: Yale University Press, 1999.

Second Vatican Council. *Dei Verbum*: *Dogmatic Constitution on Divine Revelation*. November 18, 1965.

Sen, Amartya. *Poverty and Famines: An Essay on Entitlement and Deprivation.* New York: Oxford University Press, 1981.

Shiva, Vandana. *The Violence of the Green Revolution: Third World Agriculture, Ecology and Politics.* Illustrated ed. New Jersey, NJ: Zed Books, 1991.

— *Who Really Feeds the World? The Failures of Agribusiness and the Promise of Agroecology.* Berkley, CA: North Atlantic Books, 2016.

Sideris, Lisa. *Environmental Ethics, Ecological Theology, and Natural Selection.* New York: Columbia University Press, 2003.

Smith, J. Russell. *Tree Crops: A Permanent Agriculture.* New York: The Devin-Adair, 1953.

Sollereder, Bethany N. *God, Evolution, and Animal Suffering: Theodicy without a Fall.* New York: Routledge, 2020.

Southgate, Christopher. *The Groaning of Creation: God, Evolution, and the Problem of Evil.* Louisville, KY: Westminster John Knox Press, 2008.

— "God's Creation Wild and Violent, and Our Care for Other Animals." *Perspectives on Science and Christian Faith* 67, no. 4 (2016): 245–253.

Tengö, Maria, and Kristina Belfrage. "Local Management Practices for Dealing with Change and Uncertainty: A Cross-Scale Comparison of Cases in Sweden and Tanzania." *Ecology and Society* 9, no. 3 (2004): 4. http://www.ecologyandsociety.org/vol9/iss3/art4/

Tennyson, Alfred. *In Memoriam.* New York: W.W. Norton, 2004.

Thompson, Charles D., and Melinda F. Wiggins. *The Human Cost of Food: Farmworkers' Lives, Labor, and Advocacy.* Austin, TX: University of Texas Press, 2009.

Thompson, Paul B. *The Spirit of Soil: Agriculture and Environmental Ethics.* New York: Routledge, 1994.

Toledo, Victor. "The Ecological Rationality of Peasant Production." In M. Altieri and S. B. Hecht (eds.), *Agroecology and Small Farm Development* (pp. 53–60). Boca Raton, FL: CRC Press, 1990.

— "Agroecology and Spirituality: Reflections about an Unrecognized Link." *Agroecology and Sustainable Food Systems* 46, no. 4 (2022): 626–641.

Toledo, Victor, and Narciso Barrera-Bassols. *La Memoria Biocultural: La Importancia Ecológica de Las Sabidurías Tradicionales.* Barcelona: Icaria Editorial, S.A., 2008.

Toledo, Victor, Benjamín Ortiz-Espejel, Leni Cortés, Patricia Moguel, and María de Jesús Ordoñez. "The Multiple Use of Tropical Forests by Indigenous Peoples in Mexico: A Case of Adaptive Management." *Ecology and Society* 7, no. 3 (2003): 9.

Traina, Christina L. M. "Response to Nash." In D. T. Hessel and R. Radford Ruether (eds.), *Christianity and Ecology* (pp. 251–260). Cambridge, MA: Harvard University Press, 2000.

Travieso, Emilio. "Agroecology, Aristotle, and Value(s)." Unpublished paper presented at the Oxford Department of International Development, January 19, 2015.

"Reason to Hope: Economic, Social and Ecological Virtuous Circles in Chiapas, Mexico." D.Phil thesis, University of Oxford, 2018.

UN Millennium Project. "Halving Hunger: It Can Be Done." New York: The Earth Institute at Columbia University, 2005.

United Nations Environment Programme. "Food Waste Index Report 2024. Think Eat Save: Tracking Progress to Halve Global Food Waste." Nairobi: United Nations Environment Program, 2024.

United Nations Environment Programme, International Resource Panel. "Assessing the Environmental Impacts of Consumption and Production: Priority Products and Materials," 2010. Nairobi: UNEP.

Vandermeer, John H. *The Ecology of Agroecosystems*. Sudbury, MA: Jones and Bartlett, 2011.

Vandermeer, John H., and Ivette Perfecto. *Ecological Complexity and Agroecology*. New York: Routledge, 2018.

Vandermeer, John, Meine van Noordwijk, Jo Anderson, Chin Ong, and Ivette Perfecto. "Global Change and Multi-Species Agroecosystems: Concepts and Issues." *Agriculture, Ecosystems & Environment* 67, no. 1 (1998): 1–22.

Vandermeer, John, Ivette Perfecto, and Stacy Philpott. "Ecological Complexity and Pest Control in Organic Coffee Production: Uncovering an Autonomous Ecosystem Service." *BioScience* 60, no. 7 (2010): 527–537.

Vauchez, André. *Francis of Assisi: The Life and Afterlife of a Medieval Saint*. New Haven, CT: Yale University Press, 2012.

Walker, Brian. "Conserving Biological Diversity through Ecosystem Resilience." *Conservation Biology* 9, no. 4 (1995): 747–752.

Wezel, Alexander., S. Bellon, T. Doré, et al. "Agroecology as a Science, a Movement and a Practice." *Agronomy for Sustainable Development* 29, no. 4 (2009): 503–515.

Wezel, Alexander, Barbara Gemmill Herren, Rachel Bezner Kerr, et al. "Agroecological Principles and Elements and Their Implications for

Transitioning to Sustainable Food Systems: A Review." *Agronomy for Sustainable Development* 40, no. 6 (2020).

Whelan, Matthew P. "The Grammar of Creation: Agriculture in the Thought of Pope Benedict XVI." In T. Winwright and J. Schaefer (eds.), *Environmental Justice and Climate Change: Assessing Pope Benedict XVI's Ecological Vision for the Catholic Church in the United States* (pp. 103–123). New York: Lexington Books, 2013.

"Imagination, Agriculture, and the Plagiarization of Nature." *Syndicate*, November 26, 2019. https://syndicate.network/symposia/theology/the-place-of-imagination/#imagination-agriculture-and-the-plagiarization-of-nature.

Blood in the Fields: Óscar Romero, Catholic Social Teaching, and Land Reform. Washington, DC: Catholic University of America Press, 2020.

"The Peril and the Promise of Agriculture: An Agroecological Reading of *Laudato si'*." In *Integral Ecology for a More Sustainable World: Dialogues with Laudato si'*. Lanham, MD: Lexington Books, 2020.

"Agroecology and Natural Law." *Journal of the Society of Christian Ethics* 40, no. 1 (2020): 127–144.

"Agroecology, Biological Control, and Catholic Social Teaching." *Modern Theology* 37, no. 2 (2021): 410–433.

"Agroecology's Moral Vision." *Agroecology and Human Values* 41, no. 2 (2024): 413–426.

"Care for Creation, Environmentalism, and Ecology." In F. C. Bauerschmidt, J. J. Buckley, J. N. Martin, and T. Pomplun (eds.), *Blackwell Companion to Catholicism*, 2nd ed. (pp. 550–564) Hoboken, NJ: Wiley-Blackwell, 2024.

Theological Foundations for Agriculture According to Laudato si', Laudato si' Research Institute, Campion Hall, University of Oxford, Oxford, July 2024.

White, Lynn. "The Historical Roots of Our Ecologic Crisis." *Science* 155, no. 3767 (1967): 1203–1207.

Wirzba, Norman. *Food and Faith: A Theology of Eating*. Cambridge: Cambridge University Press, 2011.

Agrarian Spirit: Cultivating Faith, Community, and the Land. Notre Dame: University of Notre Dame Press, 2022.

Worster, Donald. *Nature's Economy*. Cambridge: Cambridge University Press, 1995.

Yang, Bin, and Jun He. "Global Land Grabbing: A Critical Review of Case Studies across the World." *Land* 10, no. 3 (March 2021): 324.

Acknowledgements

The following work would not have been written without my Honduran friends from Las Joyas del Carballo and San Marcos. Juan Antonio, Delmy, Alex, Javier, Mila, Tina, Pedro, Lucinda, Ronny, Lady, Samuel, Hector, Rosa, Beatriz, Luis, along with many others, welcomed me into their lives and first nurtured my interest in agroecology.

It was primarily because of my Honduran friends that I pursued graduate work in agroecology at the Centro Agronómico Tropical de Investigación y Enseñanza (CATIE) in Turrialba, Costa Rica. I am grateful for my instructors there – Dietmar Stoian, Gabriela Soto, Eduardo Somarriba, J.D. Wulfhorst, and Cornelius Prins – and for my friends Fabricio Santos Diaz, Irma Juan Carlos, Claudia Marcela Porras, Monica Salazar, Noel Trejos, Lorena Estrada, and Jimmy Andino. Above all, my heartfelt gratitude goes to the Bribri and Cabécar peoples of Talamanca.

This research was generously supported by various grants and fellowships, including the St. Andrews Fellowship in Theology and Science, as well as Building Foundations in Science-Engaged Theology, led by John Perry and Meghan Page, respectively. A particularly formative experience was a summer fellowship at the Laudato si' Research Institute (LSRI) at Campion Hall, Oxford University. I extend my gratitude to Celia Deanne-Drummond, Séverine Deneulin, Timothy Howels, Peter Rožič SJ, Carlos Zepeda, and Harriet David at LSRI, as well as to Nicholas Austin SJ and Patrick Riordan SJ at Campion Hall. While at Campion, I first met Austen Ivereigh, and I also had an opportunity to become reacquainted with Emmanuel Katongole. Their passion for regenerative agriculture, as well as their own ecological conversions, have been a source of hope.

There have been many other sources of hope as well. One is Comparte, a Jesuit-affiliated network in Latin America that fosters collaboration and solidarity, addressing the realities of dispossession while embodying an alternative model of development that defends human dignity and cares for the wider created order. Emilio Travieso SJ integrated me into Comparte and remains one of the most luminous examples I know of the tendency of goodness to spread and share itself with others. At Baylor University, the Theology, Ecology, and Food Justice Program, directed by Jenny Howell, and the Sustainable Community and Regenerative Agriculture Project, led by Josh King and Stephanie Boddie, bear witness to an ecology capable of remedying the damage we have done to our common home.

Acknowledgements

Numerous friends and colleagues have discussed or read this Element, and their comments and insights have greatly improved it: Jake Abell, Jack Bell, Natalie Carnes, Carmody Grey, Victor Hinojosa, Jenny Howell, Pete Jordan, Joseph Lenow, Paul Martens, Brett McCarty, Bethany Sollereder, Jonathan Tran, Emilio Travieso, and Norman Wirzba. I also express my gratitude to Andrew Davison, editor of the Elements of Christianity and Science series at Cambridge University Press, as well as to the two anonymous reviewers of the manuscript.

Our deepest debts are often the most difficult to describe. My wife, Natalie Carnes, is my constant companion and wisest interlocutor, both in the writing of this Element and in all that matters. Sharing a life and a vocation with her is an immeasurable gift and daily reason for gratitude, as are our three daughters, Chora, Edith, and Simone. My parents, Pamela and William, gave me my name and my deepest commitments. They took their family off the beaten path, helping us discover new neighbors in the process. My dad's work in famine prevention provided the experiential and intellectual context in which my own sense of identity and vocation first awakened, and his hunger and thirst for justice continue to serve as an example. I happily dedicate what follows to him.

To my father, William, and my other agricultural teachers

Cambridge Elements

Christianity and Science

Andrew Davison
University of Cambridge

Andrew Davison is the Starbridge Associate Professor in Theology and Science at the University of Cambridge. He is Fellow of Corpus Christi College and Dean of the Chapel, and looks after the arts and humanities work of the Leverhulme Centre for Life in the Universe at the University of Cambridge.

Editorial Board
Natalie Carnes, *Baylor University*
Helen de Cruz, *St. Louis University*
Peter Harrison, *University of Queensland*
Sarah Lane Ritchie, *John Templeton Foundation*
Lisa Sideris, *University of California, Santa Barbara*
Jacob Sherman, *California Institute of Integral Studies*
Ignacio Alberto Silva, *Universidad Austral, Argentina*

About the Series
The Elements series on Christianity and Science will offer an authoritative presentation of scholarship in this interdisciplinary field of inquiry. Opening new avenues for study and research, the series will highlight several issues, notably the importance of historical scholarship for understanding the relationship between Christianity and natural science, and the vital role played by philosophy in this field today.

Cambridge Elements⁼

Christianity and Science

Elements in the Series

Eastern Orthodoxy and the Science-Theology Dialogue
Christopher C. Knight

Science-Engaged Theology
John Perry and Joanna Leidenhag

Science Fiction and Christian Theology
Victoria Lorrimar

Christianity and Agroecology
Matthew Philipp Whelan

A full series listing is available at: www.cambridge.org/EOCS

For EU product safety concerns, contact us at Calle de José Abascal, 56–1°, 28003 Madrid, Spain or eugpsr@cambridge.org.

www.ingramcontent.com/pod-product-compliance
Ingram Content Group UK Ltd.
Pitfield, Milton Keynes, MK11 3LW, UK
UKHW020327040925
462578UK00021B/472